The
Divided
West

BY JÜRGEN HABERMAS

Edited and Translated by
CIARAN CRONIN

polity

First published in German as *Der gespaltene Westen* by
Jürgen Habermas © Suhrkamp Verlag, Frankfurt am Main, 2004.
Chapter 1 first appeared in Giovanna Borradori, *Philosophy in a
Time of Terror: Dialogues with Jürgen Habermas and Jacques Derrida*
© The University of Chicago Press, 2003. Chapter 2 first appeared
in a translation by Max Pensky in *German Law Journal* 4/7 (2003):
701–8 and in *Constellations* 10/3 (2003): 364–70. Chapter 7
appeared under the title "America and the World: A Conversation
with Jürgen Habermas," translated by Jeffrey Craig Miller,
Logos 3/3 (Summer 2004).

Reprinted in 2008

Polity Press
65 Bridge Street
Cambridge CB2 1UR, UK

Polity Press
350 Main Street
Malden, MA 02148, USA

ISBN-10: 0-7456-3518-0
ISBN-13: 978-07456-3518-0
ISBN-10: 0-7456-3519-9 (pb)
ISBN-13: 978-07456-3519-9 (pb)

A catalogue record for this book is available from the British
Library.

Typeset in 11 on 13 pt Berling
by SNP Best-set Typesetter Ltd, Hong Kong
Printed and bound in The United States of America by Maple-Vail

For further information on Polity, visit our website: www.polity.co.uk

The publication of this work was supported by a grant from the
Goethe-Institut

Chapter 2, first published in the German Law Journal, Vol. 04.
No. 07, Pages 701–708, used with permission of the editors.

Chapter 7, this interview originally appeared in Logos:
A Journal of Modern Society and Culture 3.3, Summer 2004.
http://www.logosjournal.com/issue3.3habermasinterview.htm

Contents

Editor's Preface

The writings collected in this volume document the responses of one of the major social and political thinkers of our time to what are likely to be regarded by future generations as important events in world history. Since the early 1990s, when the end of the Cold War inaugurated dramatic changes in the international political landscape, Jürgen Habermas has produced important theoretical writings and numerous essays, and conducted interviews, devoted to global political issues. The underlying themes and concerns of these writings have remained consistent, even as Habermas has refined his ideas concerning law and politics above the national level and has responded to new political developments. His central theoretical preoccupation has been the articulation of a model of democratic politics beyond the nation-state that is capable of meeting the challenges of the "postnational constellation." In this connection, he has repeatedly discussed the process of European unification as a potential model for the transition from international law to cosmopolitan society which he advocates.

Habermas presents his approach to international law and politics as a critical appropriation of Kant's idea of a "cosmopolitan condition," to which the closing essay of this volume represents a further major contribution. This essay was also written as a direct response to the events – in particular, the policies pursued by the US government since September 11, 2001 – which have led to a damaging split within the West over the future direction and goals of global political governance. The remaining essays and interviews document Habermas's responses to these events as they occurred and thus set the political stage for the theoretical project developed systematically in the closing essay.

In what follows, I will offer some remarks on the theoretical and practical motivations of Habermas's cosmopolitan project as set forth in the closing essay. I will then show how they are reflected in some of the principal themes of the remaining essays and interviews and conclude with some observations on the role of the public intellectual as exemplified by the writings in this volume.

In the essay "Does the Constitutionalization of International Law Still Have a Chance?" Habermas argues that the continuation of the Kantian cosmopolitan project under current global conditions should take the form of a constitutionalization of international law. Kant's idea of a "cosmopolitan condition" must be freed from the historical and – as Habermas here emphasizes – *conceptual* ballast with which it is weighed down in Kant's own writings. Kant envisaged the creation of a cosmopolitan political order that would ultimately unite all human beings into a republican state of world citizens. He argued that this future "cosmopolitan condition" was a necessary complement to the republican national states then in their infancy and to the established international system of sovereign states if an enduring condition of world peace was to be achieved in an increasingly interconnected world. Although Habermas embraces the normative thrust of Kant's cosmopolitan vision – and, in particular, the central role it accords law – he now argues that its major weakness, and the reason for the apparent inconsistencies in Kant's treatment, is a conceptual one.[1] Kant failed to conceptualize the cosmopolitan condition in sufficiently abstract terms because he took the French Revolution as his model for understanding what was required to pacify international and global relations. Applying the social contract idea directly to relations between states, Kant concluded that the transition from an international to a cosmopolitan condition would require the creation of a single world republic enjoying a monopoly of coercive state authority.[2]

Habermas believes that Kantian cosmopolitanism can be liberated from these conceptual fetters by conceiving sovereignty in *procedural* rather than substantive terms and by rethinking the problem of the transition from an international to a cosmopolitan political order. On Habermas's communicative conception of reason, the validity of moral and political norms is tied to public procedures of communication that demand openness to the viewpoints and experiences of others and a willingness to reach agreements with them on shared interpretations of principles to regulate social interaction. The corresponding deliberative conception of democracy interprets the individual liberties and political participation rights enshrined in modern constitutions as guidelines for constructing legislative, executive, and judicial institutions in which the enactment, application, and interpretation of law is exposed to discursive examination and public scrutiny. Sovereignty thereby acquires a procedural meaning in the sense that the legitimacy of government at all levels (municipal, national, and supranational) becomes a function of how legal norms are legitimated through discursive procedures that must themselves be legally enabled or institutionalized.[3]

On this deliberative understanding of democracy, the constitution becomes an ongoing project in which the constitutional basic rights are implemented over time in legislative and adjudicative institutions which are, in turn, organized as deliberative procedures and are exposed to critical public scrutiny. The key question in the present context is how this model can be applied to political relations above the level of the state. Here Habermas departs from Kant in arguing that there is an important *disanalogy* between the problem of founding a democratic constitutional state and that of founding a cosmopolitan constitutional order that precludes a strictly parallel application of the idea of a social contract at both levels. Whereas the former problem required that untamed political power be brought under a rule of law by creating a sovereign constitutional authority, a rule of law already exists at the international level in the form of the "proto-constitution" composed of the legal instruments and institutions of international law. At this level, the challenge is to construct corresponding political institutions to lend the principles of this proto-constitution force in the face of urgent global political challenges. The cosmopolitan project, therefore, is not a straightforward continuation of the development of the constitutional state at the global level, as Kant assumed, and hence it does not imply the creation of a world state that would supersede existing states.

Of course, this conceptual argument only begins to answer the question of the viability, and hence the relevance, of Habermas's project of constitutionalizing international law under current global conditions. The theoretical and practical challenges it faces are formidable. If it is to be taken seriously, it must offer a plausible account of the scope and competences of the supranational governance institutions it advocates, how they can coexist with constitutional states and international alliances, and, importantly, how they can acquire discursive democratic legitimacy. Writing as a philosopher and social theorist, Habermas does not attempt to provide an empirical analysis of current global trends on which plausible conjectures concerning future developments could be based. His aim is rather to lend sufficient concrete substance to the cosmopolitan model that it can be seen as a plausible alternative to the major competing approaches. His justification strategy in chapter 8 is, broadly speaking, twofold: having staked out the conceptual parameters of the project of the constitutionalization of international law, he offers, on the one hand, a rough outline of the institutional architecture of a possible corresponding future global political order and, on the other, a defense of its normative substance against the main competing models.

The institutional architecture favored by Habermas would combine an empowered United Nations responsible for securing peace and promoting human rights at the *supranational* level with governance institutions based on cooperation among the major world powers to address urgent problems of regional and global concern at the *transnational* level. The result would be what he calls a "global domestic politics without a world government." Since this multilevel framework would not imply the existence of a single world government, its viability is not contingent on the world's population forming a single global *demos* with a shared political culture. But how then could the laws and policies of this global political order acquire discursive legitimacy? On the model Habermas proposes, national public spheres would remain the primary sites of democratic legitimation, and democratically elected national governments – and possibly delegates to a global parliament – would function as the main conduits of legitimation from their populations to the transnational and supranational institutions. Democratic legitimation above the national level would be the indirect product of a plurality of decentered discourses taking place in a variety of national and regional public spheres. Their summation would be an effective global public opinion informed by transnational media and mobilized by international non-governmental organizations that would find expression on suitable occasions in worldwide demonstrations (of which the mass protests against the American and British invasion of Iraq on February 15, 2003 may be the harbingers).

As regards the second strand of justification – the defense of the cosmopolitan project against the principal competing models – Habermas develops a complex historical-reconstructive argument designed to show that the constitutionalization of international law represents the logical continuation of a development extending over the past two centuries. The evolution of international law during the twentieth century, whose three main junctures were the founding of the League of Nations following World War I, the passage of the UN Charter after World War II, and the revitalization of the UN following the end of the Cold War, demonstrates that the transition from international law to a cosmopolitan constitution has acquired an independent historical momentum, notwithstanding the setbacks it suffered at each stage. The prohibition of war inspired by the devastating trench warfare of World War I represented a quantum leap in the development of international law and put the Kantian cosmopolitan project on the international political agenda for the first time. However, the weak institutional framework of the League of Nations, as a voluntary alliance of states lacking effective supranational institutions to codify and enforce the prohibition on wars of aggression, made it incapable of containing the aggressions unleashed by the rise of fascism. The legal and institutional innovations that emerged in response to the mass crimes of World War II went much farther in this respect. Even though the UN Charter was not intended to be a constitution for international relations, its major innovations lent it the prima facie features of a constitution. And although the stalemate imposed by the superpower rivalry during the Cold War meant that these innovations remained relatively ineffectual for many decades, their validity was never seriously questioned and they exercised a steady influence on ideas and mentalities.

The stagnation of the Cold War period marked the heyday of the classical competitor to the cosmopolitan project, namely, the "realist" view that international relations involve power struggles between states to which the moral ideas underlying the cosmopolitan project have no application. Although this amoral view of international relations derived much of its theoretical appeal from the transitory historical constellation of the Cold War, it continues to influence neoliberal models of international order that appeal to supposedly self-regulating global markets and it finds support in the recent interest in the ideas of the fascist constitutional theorist Carl Schmitt. Those suspicious of the active role that a reformed world organization would play as the supranational guarantor of peace and human rights may be sympathetic to Schmitt's hyperbolic argument that military actions undertaken on "humanitarian" grounds are merely masks for barbarism because the moralization of war implies a demonization of one's enemies as "evil" that tends to escalate hostilities into total war. However, against this and related "realist" critiques of a "moralization" of international relations, Habermas emphasizes that his project implies a *juridification* rather than a moralization of global peacekeeping operations. Humanitarian interventions would acquire the status of police operations and those accused of war crimes would not be stigmatized as morally evil but would enjoy the safeguards of due process accorded to defendants in normal criminal proceedings.[4]

Habermas's principal concern, however, is a new challenge to the cosmopolitan project as advanced once again by a revitalized United Nations during the 1990s (i.e., the third major juncture in the evolution of international law on Habermas's reconstruction). In question is the hegemonic liberal image of international order which would replace the commitment to an international rule of law with the "ethos" or moral values of a superpower, the United States, which uses its overwhelming military force unilaterally to impose democracy and human rights, as it interprets them, on "rogue states" and unstable global regions. Rather than engage in polemics concerning the true motives of the Bush administration, Habermas takes the neoconservative program at face value and argues that even a genuinely benevolent global hegemon committed to promoting human rights and democracy could not be certain that it was really acting in the interests of those it claimed to be protecting. In a globalized world that is too complex to be governed from a center, only deliberative decision-making procedures involving representatives of all of the populations concerned could produce the level of moral certainty required to justify military interventions to promote democracy and human rights (the only permissible exception being emergency interventions to prevent gross violations of human rights).

At the same time, Habermas rejects the revisionist reading of US foreign policy that argues that US advocacy of democracy and human rights was always a mask for the pursuit of national interests. On this "cynical" reading, the neoconservative orientation of the Bush administration would be merely a continuation of the main tradition in US foreign policy, whereas Habermas insists that it represents a revolutionary break with the dominant – though not, of course, the only – American tradition in international relations. The merits of Habermas's historical-reconstructive approach become particularly apparent as an antidote to this facile cynicism. From the presidency of Woodrow Wilson until the end of the twentieth century, he argues, US leaders, jurists, and political theorists were consistently at the forefront of initiatives to expand the legal and institutional foundations of the international political order. Accordingly, the policies of the Bush administration are not a logical continuation of the dominant strain in US foreign policy, but a fateful, revolutionary break with its better traditions. Moreover, it is imperative that future US administrations return to these traditions if progress toward the constitutionalization of international law is to be resumed. In the remaining essays and interviews in this volume, Habermas is unsparing in his criticisms of the divisive maneuvers of the Bush administration in pushing ahead with its divisive program both domestically and internationally.

The remainder of the volume provides numerous insights into the theoretical and practical motivations of Habermas's cosmopolitan project, of which just a few salient themes can be mentioned here. In addition to clarifying his positions on such important issues as terrorism, fundamentalism, tolerance, and the current international political system, in the opening interview (pp. 15ff.) Habermas provides a forceful defense of one of his deepest theoretical commitments, namely, that the rationality intrinsic to communication can foster normative consensus across cultures. Against deconstructionist skepticism concerning the possibility of transcultural understanding in general, he appeals to the hermeneutic and pragmatist insight that the idea of self-enclosed universes of meaning in which we are trapped is conceptually incoherent. Instead, the resources on which we unavoidably draw in everyday communication – for example, the structure of personal pronouns which compels us to adopt the perspective of our interlocutors in dialogue – also facilitate communication and understanding across cultural boundaries, at least in principle. Nevertheless, Habermas recognizes that communicative processes alone are powerless to overcome mutual distrust and incomprehension unless the material preconditions for mutual respect between cultures and global regions are realized. In view of its colonial past, therefore, the onus is on the West to examine its own political culture and to cooperate in overcoming the devastating global inequalities created by unfettered capitalism.

One issue that crops up repeatedly in these essays and interviews poses a particularly telling challenge for Habermas's cosmopolitan model. This is the apparent inconsistency between his positions on the NATO intervention in Kosovo in April 1999 and the US invasion of Iraq in March 2003, for which he has come in for sharp criticism. Habermas defended the NATO intervention on the grounds that it marked an important advance over the primacy accorded state sovereignty in classical international law. Because it was justified by the urgent need to protect the human rights of the Kosovo Albanians threatened with ethnic cleansing, the intervention could be interpreted as promoting the constitutionalization of international law.[5] By contrast, he criticized the invasion of Iraq as a revolutionary break with international law, even though it was also defended by appeals to human rights and the promotion of democracy in Iraq and the Middle East. These contrasting positions follow from a context-sensitive application of the cosmopolitan framework to the two cases. Although neither military operation had the authorization of the Security Council required by international law, the Kosovo intervention was justified by the obligation on all states in international law to prevent gross violations of human rights and by the fact that it was undertaken by an alliance of unquestionably liberal democratic states. The Iraq invasion, by contrast, was not required to prevent an imminent military threat or gross violation of human rights by the Iraqi government; moreover, the coalition assembled by the United States was clearly an ad hoc hegemonic construction that includes states with poor democratic and human rights credentials.

Habermas's core criticism of the Bush administration's "revolutionary" policy shift, therefore, concerns its unilateralism, its insistence on hegemonically pursuing national interests, by military force if necessary, in the name of one-sided interpretations of supposedly universal values such as "human rights" and "democracy." This policy assigns "allies" a subordinate role and treats international law as a mere reflection of relations of power. The contrast posed by the Habermasian project of constitutionalizing international law could hardly be starker. It regards international law as the medium in which relations between major powers and global regions can be integrated into a system of cooperative and deliberative institutions that would compel all sides to open their interpretations of human rights and democracy to criticism in a cooperative search for consensual legal norms to be backed up with credible sanctions.

However, the contrast between the Kosovo intervention and the Iraq invasion also reveals an important historical irony to which Habermas alludes on a number of occasions, namely, that the justifications of the various NATO allies for their participation in the Kosovo intervention already exhibited a significant divergence in normative outlook which the subsequent invasion of Iraq sharpened into a full-scale rift. Whereas the continental European countries regarded the intervention as a regrettable expedient to bridge the gap between legitimacy and effectiveness in the international law, though one that would ultimately promote the transition from international law to a cosmopolitan society, the Americans and the British saw it as a matter of imposing their liberal political system internationally. Moreover, the fact that the Americans could count on at least the verbal support of other European heads of government for their unilateral campaign in Iraq shows that the fatal fault line along which the policies of the Bush administration have split the West also marks an internal division within the European Union itself.

This brings us, finally, to one of the persistent themes of Habermas's recent political writings, the process of European unification. The essays and interviews collected here attest to the fact that, for Habermas, the European Union currently represents the crucible within which the key experiments in cosmopolitanism are being conducted.

His contributions to European political debates are shaped by his understanding of the challenges posed by economic, social, and cultural globalization for the established European democracies. Economic globalization, in particular, is inexorably undermining the ability of individual nation-states to regulate their own economies through national policy mechanisms. A major consequence is their increasing inability to extract the tax revenue needed to sustain social welfare programs and a looming crisis of legitimacy, which depends, among other things, on the role of the welfare state in cushioning the deleterious social effects of unfettered capitalism. Nation-states cannot meet the challenges of this emerging "post-national constellation" alone; in the long run they have no alternative but to unite into transnational and supranational associations and to cooperate in constructing a cosmopolitan political order.[6]

It is against this background that Habermas's harshly critical commentaries on the faltering process of political unification within the expanding European Union must be understood. Although the process of European integration has the potential to serve as a model for progress towards a "cosmopolitan condition," the European Union is riven by internal divisions related to those which have split the West over the future direction of global political governance. Those countries whose history and political traditions make their political elites more sympathetic to the Anglo-American model of liberal democracy – in particular, Great Britain and the Scandinavian countries – tend to favor a model of European integration based on economic liberalization. They accordingly seek to limit the competences of European institutions and agencies to matters of market regulation and jealously defend the sovereignty of member states in such sensitive areas as social, defense, and foreign policy. By contrast, the vision of a united Europe shared by the Western European founding countries – France, Germany, Italy, and the Benelux countries – remains deeply influenced by the ideals of the post-war generation, which regarded a future united Europe as necessary to overcome the disastrous historical antagonisms between the European states.[7] The festering conflict between these opposing visions reached new heights in the recent controversy over a constitution for the EU that is urgently needed to cope with the problems of governing a Union whose enlargement is aggravating the already acute "democratic deficit" of the EU institutions.[8]

Among Habermas's most important contributions to European debates are those that focus on the preconditions of democracy at the European level and of a corresponding European political identity and culture.[9] Against those who claim that there cannot be a European democracy because there is no European *demos* that could function as the subject of popular sovereignty, he argues that a shared political identity is not a prior condition of democratic legitimation, but is constituted through the process of translating constitutional basic rights into law within an enfolding constitutional project. Such a project is viable provided that the populations concerned share sufficient commonalities to foster the solidarity required to support mutual sacrifices. On the deliberative understanding of democracy, a procedurally generated "constitutional patriotism" replaces the idea of a shared descent and culture beloved of nationalists as the focus and medium of political identification.

In chapter 3, Habermas argues that Europeans possess a sufficiently rich store of common political values and traditions to make a deeper constitutionalization of the Union possible. An important refinement here is his argument that new organizational tasks and the requirements of redistribution across wider geographical spaces entailed by the eastern enlargement will inevitably generate increased demands for broader citizen participation in European decision-making. This necessitates a corresponding deepening of mutual solidarity and identification, and this can only be insured by a deeper political integration of the Union. Democratization at the supra-national level, by contrast, entails comparatively modest demands on global solidarity because the tasks of a reformed United Nations would be restricted to peace-keeping and protecting human rights. At this level, a shared sense of outrage at gross violations of human rights, whose existence is already attested by spontaneous pro-tests, would be sufficient to invest the actions of the world organization with democratic legitimacy.

Taken as a whole, these writings invite us to reflect, in conclusion, on the relation between Habermas's enact-ment of the role of public intellectual in his interventions in political debates and the function his cosmopolitan model assigns a transnational public sphere in fostering democracy above the national level. Although Habermas writes in the first instance as a German philosopher and social theorist addressing a German educated public, in which role he has frequently had a major influence on public opinion in post-war Germany, he is also acutely aware of the need for a transnational networking of public discourse in the emerging postnational constellation. The appeal documented by the essay "February 15, or: What Binds Europeans" is particularly interesting in this regard. The essay, which was co-signed by Jacques Derrida, was Habermas's contribution to an initiative in which he invited a number of prominent European and American intellectuals to join in responding to the clearly expressed intention of the US government to attack Iraq come what may. This initiative can be interpreted as a contribution to promoting the horizontal networking of national public spheres called for by Habermas's model of transnational deliberative democratic legitimation, and hence as a discursive counterpart to the spontaneous mass demon-strations against the imminent invasion of Iraq in major European cities and across the world on February 15, 2003.

Here Habermas is writing as a European intellectual, as the proponent of a vanguard role for the "core" founding member states of the European Union in reviving the stalled process of European unification, and as an advocate of the shared values on which a European political identity and culture could be founded. In the emerging global constellation, a united and self-confident Europe represents for Habermas the most viable political, if not military, alternative to hegemonic unilateralism and the best safeguard against a new era of major power rivalry – or a new balance of threats between hostile "hemispheres" – as the inevitable pretenders emerge to challenge the current military supremacy of the United States.

Ciaran Cronin

Author's Foreword

The West was not divided by the danger of international terrorism but by policies of the current US government that ignore international law, marginalize the United Nations and accept the inevitability of the break with Europe. What is at stake is the Kantian project of abolishing the state of nature between states. The source of disagreement is not the apparent political goals but one of the greatest efforts to advance human civilization. The concluding essay in this book is intended to draw attention to this fact.

Of course, the split also runs through Europe and America themselves. In Europe, it mainly troubles those who have identified throughout their lives with the best American traditions, with the roots of the political Enlightenment around the turn of the nineteenth century, the rich currents of pragmatism and the return to internationalism after 1945.

For Germans, the blatant repudiation of these traditions serves as a litmus test. The chemical bond formed by Germany's turn to the West since Adenauer is now disintegrating into its two constituent elements. The moral and intellectual identification with the principles and basic commitments of Western culture, to which a finally liberalized Germany owes its normative self-understanding, is detaching itself unmistakably from

Germany's opportunistic accommodation to the hegemonic power which took Europe under its atomic umbrella during the Cold War.

I want to draw attention to this difference as well. The study on the constitutionalization of international law provides an opportunity to bring together some previously published writings which throw light on the relation between this question and the goal of European unification.

Jürgen Habermas
Starnberg

Note on the Translation

A number of the interviews and essays in this volume were previously published in translation and appear here in revised form. Chapter 1 appeared under the same title in a translation by Luiz Guzman in Giovanna Borradori, *Philosophy in a Time of Terror: Dialogues with Jürgen Habermas and Jacques Derrida* (Chicago: University of Chicago Press, 2003). Chapter 2 appeared in a translation by Max Pensky in *German Law Journal* 4/7 (2003): 701–8 and in *Constellations* 10/3 (2003): 364–70. Chapter 7 appeared under the title "America and the World: A Conversation with Jürgen Habermas," translated by Jeffrey Craig Miller, *Logos* 3/3 (Summer 2004). The translation of the final essay incorporates numerous textual revisions by the author.

After September 11

1
Fundamentalism and Terror[1]

Question: Do you consider what we now tend to call "September 11" an unprecedented event, one that radically alters the way we see ourselves?

J. H.: Let me say in advance that I am answering your questions at a distance of three months. Thus, it may be useful to mention my personal experiences of the event. Since the beginning of October, I have once again spent about two months in Manhattan. I must confess that this time I somehow felt more of a stranger than on any previous visit to the "capital of the twentieth century," a city that has fascinated me for more than three decades. Not just the flag-waving and somewhat defiant "United We Stand" patriotism had altered the climate, nor just the unaccustomed demand for solidarity and the associated touchiness concerning any presumed "anti-Americanism." The impressive American generosity toward foreigners, the charm of the eager, sometimes even self-consciously overbearing embrace – this wonderfully openhearted mentality seemed to have given way to a certain mistrust. It was as if people were asking themselves whether we who had not been present would now also stand by them unconditionally. Even those who have an indubitable "record," as I do among my American friends, had to be careful with criticism. Since the intervention in

Afghanistan, I suddenly began to notice when I found myself among Europeans (or among Europeans and Israelis) in political discussions.

On the other hand, only at the scene of the event did I fully appreciate its magnitude. I experienced the outrage over this disaster, which came literally as a bolt out of the blue, the contemptible convictions which motivated this treacherous assault and the stifling depression which descended on the city in a completely different way from at home. Every friend and colleague could remember exactly what they were doing that morning just after 9.00 a.m. In other words, only at the scene itself did I begin to comprehend better the mood of foreboding which still reverberates in your question. Even among the Left there is a widespread sense of living at a turning point in history. I don't know whether the US government itself was some-what paranoid or merely shirking responsibility. At any rate, the repeated and utterly vague announcements of possible new terror attacks and the senseless appeal to "be alert" exacerbated the vague sense of dread and the indefinite state of alarm – in other words, precisely what the terrorists intended. In New York people seemed ready for the worst. The anthrax attacks (and even the plane crash in Queens) were attributed to Osama bin Laden's diabolical machinations almost as a matter of course.[2]

Given this background, you can appreciate a certain skepticism on my part. Is what we contemporaries currently think really all that important for a long-term diagnosis? If the September 11 terror attack is supposed to represent a caesura in "world history," as many think, then it has to withstand comparison with other events of world historical moment. August 1914, not Pearl Harbor, provides the most appropriate comparison. The outbreak of World War I signaled the end of a peaceful and, in retrospect, somewhat naive period. It unleashed an era of total warfare, totalitarian oppression, mechanized barbarity, and bureaucratic mass murder. At the time, a sense of foreboding was widespread. Only with hindsight will we

4

be able to determine whether the symbolically charged collapse of the capitalistic citadels in Lower Manhattan represents such a profound break or whether this catastrophe merely confirms, in a dramatically inhuman way, a long-recognized vulnerability of our complex civilization. When we are dealing with historical events of less manifest import than the French Revolution – Kant immediately spoke of it as a "historical sign" pointing to a "moral tendency of humankind" – only the historical effects can decide as to their magnitude.

Perhaps later, it will be possible to trace important developments back to September 11. However, we do not know which of the many future scenarios currently circulating will actually transpire. The cleverly constructed, though fragile, coalition against terrorism assembled by the US government could, on the best-case scenario, promote the transition from classical international law to a cosmopolitan order. At least a hopeful signal was sent out by the Afghanistan conference in Bonn under the auspices of the UN, which pointed the agenda in the right direction.[3] However, the European governments have failed utterly following September 11. They are clearly incapable of seeing beyond their narrow national interests and at least lending their support to someone like Colin Powell against the hard-liners. The Bush administration seems set to continue more or less unperturbed the course of a self-centered, obdurate superpower. As in the past, it continues to resist the appointment of an international criminal court, relying instead on military tribunals of its own, which are contrary to international law. It refuses to sign the Biological Weapons Convention. It unilaterally terminated the ABM Treaty and absurdly sees its plan to deploy a missile defense system as validated by the events of September 11. The world has grown too complex for this thinly veiled unilateralism. Even if Europe does not pull itself together and play its appointed civilizing role, the emerging global power China and the waning power Russia will not so readily accommodate themselves to the *pax Americana* model. Instead of the kind of international police operation we had hoped for during the war in Kosovo, we have, once again, old-fashioned wars, albeit conducted with state-of-the-art technology.

The misery in war-torn Afghanistan is reminiscent of images from the Thirty Years War. Of course, there were good reasons, indeed good normative reasons, to overthrow the Taliban regime, which brutally oppressed not just women but the entire population. It opposed the legitimate demand to hand over bin Laden. However, the asymmetry between the concentrated destructive power of the clusters of elegant, electronically guided missiles in the air and the archaic ferocity of the swarms of bearded warriors equipped with Kalashnikovs on the ground remains a morally obscene spectacle. This strikes home when one recalls Afghanistan's murderous colonial history, its arbitrary geographic division, and its continued instrumentalization by the major powers. The Taliban, at any rate, has been consigned to history.

Question: True, but our topic is terrorism, which seems to have taken on a new meaning and character since September 11.

J. H.: The monstrosity of the act was new. And I don't just mean the action of the suicidal hijackers who transformed the fully fueled airplanes along with their hostages into living missiles, nor even the unspeakable number of victims and the dramatic extent of the devastation. What was new was the symbolic force of the targets struck. The attackers not only physically demolished the tallest buildings in Manhattan; they also destroyed an icon in the collective store of images of the American nation. Only through the surge of patriotism which followed could one grasp the central importance that this striking silhouette on the Manhattan skyline, this powerful embodiment of economic strength and aspirations for the future, had acquired in the imagination of an entire people. Also new was the presence of cameras and the media, which transformed the local event in real time into a global one and the whole world into a benumbed witness. Perhaps September 11 could be called the first world-historical event in a strict sense: the impact, the explosion, the slow collapse – all of which was unfortunately no longer Hollywood but a horrific reality – literally unfolded before the eyes of a global public. God only knows what my friend and colleague experienced as he watched the second airplane crash into the top floors of the World Trade Center just a few blocks from the roof of his house on Duane Street. No doubt it was something completely different from what I experienced in Germany in front of the television, though we saw the same thing.

However, no observations of a unique event alone can explain why terrorism itself should have assumed a new character. In this respect, one factor above all seems to me to be relevant: we don't really know who the enemy is. Osama bin Laden, the person, serves more as a stand-in. Compare the new terrorists with guerrillas or conventional terrorists, in Israel, for example. These people also often operate in a decentralized manner in small, independent units. In these cases, too, no concentration of forces or central organization exists that could serve as an easy target. But guerrillas fight on familiar territory with professed political objectives and with the aim of seizing power. This is what distinguishes them from terrorists who are scattered around the globe and are networked like secret services. The latter declare, at most, religious motives of a fundamentalist kind but do not pursue any program beyond engineering destruction and insecurity. The terrorism we associate for the present with the name "al-Qaeda" makes the identification of the opponent and any realistic assessment of the risk impossible. This intangibility lends the terrorism a new quality.

7

To be sure, the indeterminacy of the danger belongs to the essence of terrorism. But the scenarios of biological or chemical warfare painted in detail by the American media during the months following September 11 and the speculations concerning the different kinds of nuclear terrorism merely betray the inability of the government to determine at least the magnitude of the risk. No one knows whether there's anything to it. In Israel, people at least know *what* can happen to them if they take a bus, go into a department store, discotheque, or any open area – and *how frequently it happens*. In the USA and Europe, it's impossible to circumscribe the risk; there's no realistic way to estimate the type, magnitude, and probability of the risk or to narrow down the potentially affected regions.

This leaves a threatened nation, which can react to such uncertain dangers only through administrative channels, in the embarrassing position of possibly overreacting, yet without being able to know whether it is overreacting because of the inadequacy of intelligence information. For this reason, the state runs the risk of being discredited by the inappropriateness of the measures it deploys, whether internally by a militarization of security that undermines the rule of law or externally by mobilizing a disproportionate and ineffective military and technological supremacy. US Secretary of Defense Donald Rumsfeld again warned, with pretty transparent motives, of *unspecified* terror threats at the NATO conference in Brussels in mid-December: "As we look at the devastation they unleashed in the US, contemplate the destruction they could wreak in New York, or London, or Paris or Berlin with nuclear, chemical or biological weapons."[4] Of a rather different kind were the measures – necessary and prudent, but only effective in the long term – which the US government undertook immediately following the attack: the creation of a worldwide coalition of countries against terrorism, the effective monitoring of suspicious financial transfers and international banking connections, the networking of relevant information flows among national intelligence

8

agencies, as well as the worldwide coordination of corresponding police investigations.

Question: You have claimed that the intellectual is a figure with historically specific characteristics, deeply intertwined with European history, the nineteenth century, and the onset of modernity. Does he or she play a particular role in our present context?

J. H.: I wouldn't say so. Those who usually speak out on such occasions – writers, philosophers, artists, academics in the humanities and the social sciences – have done so this time, too. There have been the usual pros and cons, the same confusion of voices with the familiar national differences in style and public resonance – not much different from the Gulf War or the Kosovo War, in fact. Perhaps the American voices were somewhat hastier and louder than usual – and ultimately rather more patriotic and ready to toe the official line. Even liberals on the Left seem to agree with Bush's policies for the moment. Richard Rorty's clear-cut positions are, if I am correct, not completely atypical. On the other hand, critics of the military operation in Afghanistan started from a false prognosis in their practical assessment of its chances for success. On this occasion, what was needed was not only anthropological and historical knowledge of a somewhat specialized kind but also military and geopolitical expertise. Not that I would subscribe to the anti-intellectual prejudice that intellectuals frequently lack the required expert knowledge. If you are not an economist, then you refrain from making judgments on complex economic matters. With regard to military matters, however, intellectuals clearly behave no differently from other armchair strategists.

Question: In your Paulskirche speech (Frankfurt, October 2001), you defined fundamentalism as a specifically modern phenomenon.[5] Why?

9

J. H.: It depends, of course, on how you want to use the term. "Fundamentalist" has a pejorative ring to it. We use this adjective to characterize a mindset that stubbornly insists on the political imposition of its own convictions and reasons, even when they are far from being generally acceptable. This holds especially for religious beliefs. However, we should not confuse dogmatism and ortho-doxy with fundamentalism. Every religious doctrine rests on a dogmatic kernel of belief. Sometimes there is an authority like the Pope, or the Roman Catholic Congrega-tion for the Doctrine of the Faith, which determines what interpretations deviate from this dogma and hence from orthodoxy. Such orthodoxy only becomes fundamentalist when the guardians and representatives of the true faith ignore the epistemic situation of a pluralistic society and insist – even to the point of violence – on the universal validity and political imposition of their doctrine.

Until the onset of modernity, the prophetic teachings which emerged during the Axial Age[6] were also *world* religions in the sense that they were able to expand within the cognitive horizons of the ancient empires, which appeared from within to be all-encompassing worlds. The "universalism" of those empires, whose peripheries seemed to extend without limit when viewed from the center, provided a suitable background for the exclusive claim to truth of the world religions. However, under the modern conditions of an accelerated growth in complexity, such an exclusive claim to truth by one faith can no longer be naively upheld. In Europe, the confessional schism and the secularization of society compelled religious faiths to reflect on their non-exclusive status within a universe of discourse shared with other religions and constrained by secular scientific knowledge. At the same time, the reflexive awareness of this double relativization of one's own position obviously does not mean that one should relativize one's beliefs. This self-reflexive accomplishment of a religion that learned to see itself through the eyes of others had important political implications. The believers could thenceforth grasp why they had to renounce violence in general, and recourse to state power in particular, to enforce their religious claims. This cognitive impulse first made religious tolerance and the separation between state and church possible.

When a contemporary regime like Iran refuses to accept this separation, or when religiously inspired movements strive to re-establish an Islamic form of theocracy, we regard this as fundamentalism. I would explain this obdurate fanaticism in terms of the repression of cognitive dissonances. This repression becomes necessary when the epistemological innocence of an all-encompassing worldview has long since been lost and a return to the exclusivity of pre-modern outlooks is advocated under the cognitive conditions of scientific knowledge and religious pluralism. These attitudes cause such striking cognitive dissonances because the complex conditions of life in modern pluralistic societies are normatively compatible only with a *strict* universalism that demands equal respect for everybody, be they Catholic, Protestant, Muslim, Jewish, Hindu, or Buddhist, believers or non-believers.

Question: How is the kind of Islamic fundamentalism we see today different from earlier fundamentalist trends and practices, such as the witch-hunts of the early modern age?

J. H.: There is probably one motif that links the two phenomena you mention, namely, the defensive reaction against the fear of a violent disruption of traditional ways of life. In the early modern age, the beginnings of political and economic modernization may have given rise to such fears in some parts of Europe. Of course, with the globalization of markets, in particular of financial markets, and with the expansion of foreign direct investments, we find ourselves today at a completely different stage. Things are

11

also different in that world society has in the meantime *split up* into winner, beneficiary, and loser countries. To the Arab world, the US is the driving force of capitalist modernization. With its unchallengeable lead in development and its crushing technological, economic, political, and military superiority, the US represents both an affront to its self-confidence and a secretly admired ideal. The West as a whole serves as a scapegoat for the Arab world's own very real experiences of loss, suffered by a population uprooted from its cultural traditions by radically accelerated processes of modernization. What Europeans experienced under more favorable conditions as a process of *creative* destruction does not, in other countries, hold out the promise of compensation for the pain caused by the disintegration of customary ways of life. People lack a sense that this compensation can even be achieved within the horizon of foreseeable generations.

It is understandable on a psychological level that this defensive reaction should be nourished by spiritual sources that seem to involve a potential to resist the secularizing force of the West that the latter has lost sight of. The enraged fundamentalist recourse to a form of faith that modernity has taught neither to become self-reflexive nor to distinguish between religion, secular knowledge, and politics, acquires a certain plausibility from the fact that it feeds on resources that the West seems to lack. The West confronts other cultures, which owe their character to the imprint of one of the great world religions, only through the provocative and trivializing aura of a banal materialistic consumerist culture. Let's admit it – the West presents itself in a form bereft of any normative core as long as its concern for human rights only extends to promoting free markets abroad, and it allows free rein to the neoconservative division of labor between religious fundamentalism and a kind of vacuous secularization at home.

Question: Philosophically speaking, do you consider terrorism to be a wholly political act?

12

J. H.: Not in the subjective sense in which Mohammed Atta, the Egyptian national from Hamburg who piloted the first of the airplanes involved in the catastrophe, would offer you a political answer. However, today's Islamic fundamentalism is no doubt always also a product of political motives. At any rate, we should not overlook the political motives that we are today encountering in the form of religious fanaticism. This explains the fact that many of the terrorists now engaging in the "holy war" were secular nationalists just a few years ago. If you look at the biographies of these people, you find striking continuities. Disappointment over nationalistic military regimes may have contributed to the fact that religion currently offers a new, and clearly subjectively more convincing, language for the old political orientations.

Question: How would you actually define terrorism? Can a meaningful distinction be drawn between national and international, or even global, terrorism?

J. H.: In one respect Palestinian terrorism remains old-fashioned. It revolves around murder and homicide, the indiscriminate annihilation of enemies, women, and children – a life for a life. This is different from the terror that takes the form of paramilitary guerrilla warfare. The latter was characteristic of many national liberation movements in the latter half of the twentieth century and has left its mark on the current Chechnyan struggle for independence, for example. The global terror that culminated in the September 11 attacks, by contrast, exhibits the anarchistic traits of an impotent revolt against an enemy that cannot be defeated in any pragmatic sense. Its only possible effect is to shock and alarm the government and population. Technically speaking, our complex societies offer ideal opportunities for concerted disruptions of normal activities because they are highly susceptible to interferences and accidents. These disruptions can produce major destructive effects with a minimum of effort.

13

Global terrorism is extreme both in its lack of realistic goals and in its cynical exploitation of the vulnerability of complex systems.

Question: Should terrorism be distinguished from ordinary crimes and other types of violence?

J. H.: Yes and no. From a moral point of view, there is no excuse for terrorist acts, regardless of their motive or the situation in which they are carried out. Nothing justifies our "taking for granted" the murder or suffering of others to promote our own ends. Each murder is one too many. Historically, however, terrorism falls under a different category from the kinds of crimes that concern a criminal court. It differs from private matters in that it merits public interest and demands a different kind of analysis from that of murder committed out of jealousy, for example. Otherwise, we would not be having this interview. The difference between political terror and ordinary crime becomes clear when regime changes bring former terrorists to power and transform them into respected representatives of their countries. Certainly, terrorists can only hope for such a political transition if they pursue coherent political goals in a realistic manner, and hence can draw a certain, at least retrospective, legitimation for their criminal actions as endeavors to overcome a manifestly unjust situation. However, I cannot presently imagine any context that could one day somehow make the monstrous crime of September 11 an understandable and comprehensible political act.

Question: Do you think it was a good idea to interpret this act as a declaration of war?

J. H.: Even if the term "war" is less misleading and morally less dubious than "crusade," I consider Bush's decision to call for a "war against terrorism" a serious normative and pragmatic error. Normatively speaking, he is elevating

14

these criminals to the status of enemies in war and, as a pragmatic matter, one cannot conduct a war against an elusive "network" if the term "war" is to retain any precise meaning.

Question: If the West needs to develop greater sensitivity and become more self-critical in its dealings with other cultures, how should it go about doing that? Philosophically, you have articulated the interrelation between "translation" and the "search for a common language." Can this be the key to a new political course?

J. H.: Since September 11, people have often asked me whether, in light of such manifestations of violence, the whole conception of "communicative action" developed in the *Theory of Communicative Action* has not been discredited. To be sure, even in our peaceful and well-to-do OECD societies we have in a sense become accustomed to the *structural* violence of invidious social inequalities, of humiliating discrimination, and of impoverishment and marginalization. Precisely because our social relations are pervaded by violence, strategic action, and manipulation, we should not overlook two additional facts. On the one hand, our daily social practice rests on a solid basis of common background convictions, taken-for-granted cultural truths and mutual expectations. At this level, the coordination of action takes place via familiar language games and mutual, and at least implicitly recognized, validity claims *in the public space of more or less good reasons*. On the other hand, this means that conflicts arise due to *disruptions in communication*, from misunderstanding and incomprehension, insincerity and deception. When these conflicts become painful enough, they end up in court or on the therapist's couch. The spiral of violence begins with a spiral of disrupted communication that leads through a spiral of unchecked mutual mistrust to the breakdown of communication. However, if violence begins with disruptions in communication, once it has erupted it is possible to determine what went wrong and what needs to be repaired.

We can also apply this mundane insight to the conflicts to which you refer. Things are more complicated in this case because different cultures, ways of life, and nations are more distant from and, hence, more foreign to one another. They do not encounter each other like family members or fellow-countrymen who first become *estranged* from each other through systematically distorted communication. Furthermore, in *international* relations the deterrent power of the law plays a comparatively weak role. And in *intercultural* relations the legal system can at best create an institutional framework for attempts at formal communication, such as the UN Conference on Human Rights in Vienna. As important as the multilevel intercultural discourse concerning the controversial interpretation of human rights may be, such formal encounters cannot break out of the spiral of stereotyping by themselves. Rather, mentalities are transformed through improvements in living conditions, through perceptible relief from oppression and fear. A reserve of trust must be able to develop in everyday communication. Only then can a broadly effective process of enlightenment extend into the media, schools, and homes. And it must start with the premises of one's own political culture.

In this context, how we represent ourselves toward other cultures becomes important for ourselves, too. Through such a revision of its self-image, for example, the West could learn how it would need to change its policies if it wants to be seen as a *civilizing* force. Unless unfettered capitalism is tamed, the devastating stratification of world society will remain intractable. The most destructive disparities in the dynamics of economic development would have to be at least balanced out – I'm thinking of the deprivation and impoverishment of whole regions and continents. It is not just a matter of discrimination and the denigration and humiliation of other cultures. The so-called "clash of civilizations" is often just a disguise for the concrete material interests of the West (for example, access to oil reserves and securing the energy supply).

Question: In light of what you are suggesting, shouldn't we ask ourselves whether the dialogue model suits the intercultural exchange at all? Don't we always invoke the solidarity between cultures in our own terms?

J. H.: The persistent deconstructivist suspicion of Euro-centric prejudices invites a counter-question: why should the hermeneutic model of understanding, which is derived from everyday conversation and, since Humboldt, has been methodologically refined from the practice of textual interpretation, suddenly break down at the boundaries of our own culture, of our own way of life and traditions? Interpretations always have to bridge the gap between the hermeneutic pre-understanding of each side, whether the cultural and spatiotemporal distances are shorter or longer and the semantic differences smaller or larger. All inter-pretations are translations *in nuce*. We don't have to appeal to a Donald Davidson to understand that the idea of a conceptual scheme that constitutes one world among many involves a contradiction. One can also use Gadame-rian arguments to show that the idea of a self-contained universe of meanings that is incommensurable with other universes of this type is inconsistent.

However, this does not necessarily entail a methodical ethnocentrism. Richard Rorty and Alasdair MacIntyre defend an "assimilation model" of understanding whereby radical interpretation means either assimilation to one's own standards of rationality or a conversion and, hence, a kind of subjection to the rationality of a completely alien view of the world. On this view, we can understand only what accords with the dictates of a world-disclosing language. However, this description fits at best the very beginning of an interpretation, a perplexing situation that demands hermeneutic effort because it makes participants painfully aware of the one-sided nature and

17

limitations of their initial conjectures. In struggling with the difficulties of understanding, participants in conversation must progressively broaden their original perspectives until they finally achieve congruence. Moreover, they can achieve such a "fusion of horizons" in virtue of their ability to assume the roles of "speaker" and "hearer" through which they engage in a fundamental symmetry that all speech situations ultimately demand. Every competent speaker has learned how to use the system of personal pronouns and has thereby acquired competence in switching between the first and second persons. And in the course of mutual perspective taking, a common horizon of background assumptions can develop in which both sides reach an interpretation that is neither ethnocentrically condescending nor a conversion, but something *intersubjectively* shared.

Moreover, this hermeneutic model explains why attempts at understanding can only succeed under symmetrical conditions of *mutual* perspective taking. Good intentions and the absence of naked force are, of course, helpful, but they are not sufficient. Without the structures of a communicative situation free from distortion and latent power relations, the results are always open to the suspicion of being imposed. Of course, most of the time the selectivity and the need for revision of the interpretations obtained merely reflect the inevitable fallibility of the human mind. However, such normal failures are often indistinguishable from the element of blindness which interpretations owe to the persistent traces of forced submission to the will of the stronger. Hence, communication is always ambiguous and always also an expression of latent violence. But when this description of communication is ontologized, when one sees "nothing but" violence in it, one misses the essential point, namely, that the critical power to put a stop to violence without reproducing it in new forms can only dwell in the telos of mutual understanding and our orientation to this goal.

Question: Globalization has brought us to reconsider the international law concept of sovereignty. How do you see the role of international organizations in relation to it? Does cosmopolitanism, one of the central ideals of the Enlightenment, still play a useful role in today's circumstances?

J. H.: I regard Carl Schmitt's existentialist notion that "the political" consists merely in the self-assertion of a collective identity over and against other collective identities as false and, in view of its practical consequences, dangerous. For the ontologization of the friend–foe relation implies that attempts to juridify relations between the belligerent subjects of international law at the global level always merely serve to dress up particular interests in universalistic garb. Yet, we cannot simply ignore the fact that the horrendous mass crimes of the totalitarian regimes of the twentieth century have definitively refuted the presumption of innocence of states in classical international law. For this historical reason, we have long since begun the transition from classical international law to what Kant foresaw as a "cosmopolitan condition." This is a fact; moreover, normatively speaking, I do not see any coherent alternative to such a development. However, we should not overlook the obverse side of this transition, for a whole series of developments has revealed its ambivalence with increasing clarity. I am thinking of the Nuremberg and Tokyo war crimes tribunals following World War II, the founding of the United Nations and the adoption of the UN Declaration of Human Rights, the more active human rights policy pursued since the end of the Cold War, the controversial NATO intervention in Kosovo, and, currently, the declaration of war against international terrorism.

On the one hand, the idea of an international community that brings to an end the state of nature between nations by effectively penalizing wars of aggression, genocide, and crimes against humanity, and punishing

19

violations of human rights, has taken institutional shape in the UN and its various branches. The tribunal in The Hague is currently hearing the case against Slobodan Milosevic, a former head of state. The top British judges almost prevented the repatriation of Augusto Pinochet, a criminal ex-dictator. The establishment of an international criminal court is under way. The principle of non-intervention in the domestic affairs of sovereign states has been undermined. Resolutions of the Security Council have revoked the Iraqi government's freedom to use its own airspace. UN peacekeepers are guaranteeing the safety of the post-Taliban government in Kabul. Moreover, Macedonia, which was on the brink of a civil war, has acceded to demands of the Albanian minority under pressure from the EU.

On the other hand, the world organization is often little more than a paper tiger. It depends on the cooperation of the major powers. The Security Council can ensure only very selective compliance with the avowed principles of the international community, even after the events of 1989. UN troops are often unable to meet UN guarantees, as the Srebrenica tragedy demonstrates. When the decisions of the Security Council are blocked, as in the Kosovo conflict, and when a regional alliance like NATO acts in its place without a mandate, the fatal power differential between the legitimate but weak authority of the international community and the military capability of nation-states acting in their own interests becomes apparent.

The discrepancy between ought and can, between law and power, undermines both the credibility of the UN and the practice of intervention by unauthorized states which merely usurps a mandate – though perhaps for good reasons – and thereby debases a would-be legitimate police action into an act of war. For the would-be police action then becomes indistinguishable from a run-of-the-mill war. This confused mixture of classical power politics, deference toward regional allies, and the beginnings of a cosmopolitan legal regime not only reinforces the existing conflicts of interest between North and South and East and West within the UN. It also fosters the mistrust of the superpower toward all normative constraints on its room for maneuver. This, in turn, leads to increasing contention within the Western camp between the Anglo-Saxon and continental countries. The former draw their inspiration from the "realistic school" of international relations, whereas the latter favor a normative legitimation tied to an accelerated transformation of international law into a cosmopolitan legal order.

During the war in Kosovo, and even in policy toward Afghanistan, one could clearly discern corresponding differences in the respective agendas and goals. This tension between more pragmatic and more normative goals will only be resolved if one day the major continental alliances, like the EU, NAFTA, and ASEAN, develop into empowered actors capable of reaching transnational agreements and assuming responsibility for an ever-denser transnational network of organizations, conferences, and practices. Only such global players capable of forming a political counterweight to the unchecked global expansion of markets running ahead of any political framework could provide the UN with a basis for implementing high-minded programs and policies.

Question: Many have admired the universalism you defend in your writings on moral and political philosophy; many have criticized it. What does this universalism have to do with tolerance? Is tolerance not a paternalistic term that would be better off being replaced by the concept of "hospitality" or "friendship"?

J. H.: Historically, the concept of tolerance has certainly had this connotation. Think, for example, of the Edict of Nantes by which the French king permitted the Huguenots, a religious minority, to profess their beliefs and practice their observances provided that they did not question royal authority or the supremacy of Catholicism.

21

Tolerance has been practiced for centuries in this paternalistic spirit. What renders it paternalistic is the one-sided nature of the declaration that a sovereign ruler or the majority culture is willing, at its own discretion, to "put up with" the deviant practices of the minority. In this context, the act of toleration retains the connotation of a burden, an act of mercy or "granting a favor." One party allows the other a certain amount of deviation from "normality" on one condition: that the tolerated minority does not overstep the "boundary of tolerance." This authoritarian "permission conception" of tolerance (Rainer Forst) has been justly criticized, for it is obvious that the threshold of tolerance which separates what is still "acceptable" from what is not is set arbitrarily by the reigning authority. This can give the impression that tolerance itself involves a kernel of intolerance, since one can only practice it within a boundary beyond which it ceases. This, though, seems to be what underlies your question.

Today, for example, we encounter this paradox in the concept of "militant democracy": no freedom for the enemies of freedom. However, this example also shows that the complete deconstruction of the concept of tolerance falls into a trap. For the constitutional state contradicts the very premise from which the traditional, paternalistic concept of "tolerance" is derived. Within a democratic community whose citizens reciprocally accord each other equal rights, there is no room for an authority that could *unilaterally* determine the boundaries of what should be tolerated. Given citizens' equal rights and mutual respect for each other, nobody has the privilege of defining the limits of tolerance exclusively from the perspective of his or her own preferences and value-orientations. Certainly, tolerating each other's beliefs without accepting their truth, and tolerating each other's ways of life while regarding them as less valuable than one's own, require a standard based on shared values. However, in the case of a democratic community, the latter are enshrined in the principles of justice of the constitution. Of course, disputes arise over the proper understanding of these norms and principles too. What is important, however, is the peculiar reflexive character that constitutional principles enjoy. This complex issue brings us back to the question of universalism.

The constitution itself makes the necessary provisions for resolving conflicts over the interpretation of the constitution. It lays down institutions and procedures for settling where the line should be drawn between cases that can still, and those that can no longer, count as remaining "loyal to the constitution." This applies in particular to the kind of public agitation that sets itself beyond the "pale" of the constitution (as currently with Islamic extremism). Interestingly, in a community that tolerates "civil disobedience," constitutional protection also extends beyond these procedures, even beyond all the practices and institutions in which its own normative content has been spelled out and has acquired binding force. By tolerating civil disobedience, the constitution can even extend self-reflexively to include the conditions for transgressing its own boundaries. A democratic constitution also tolerates the resistance of dissidents who, having exhausted all legal avenues, nonetheless oppose legitimate decisions or judgments. It only imposes the condition that this rule-transgressing resistance be plausibly justified in accordance with the spirit and wording of the constitution and be conducted by symbolic means that lend the struggle the character of a non-violent appeal to the majority to once again reflect on their decisions. In this way, the democratic project of realizing equal civil rights actually feeds off the resistance of minorities, which, although they appear to be enemies of democracy to the majority today, *could* prove to be its true friends tomorrow.

To return to your question, this reflexive self-transcendence of the boundaries of tolerance of a "militant democracy" is a function of the universalistic nature of the legal and moral foundations of a liberal order. For only the egalitarian individualism of a rational morality that demands mutual recognition, in the sense of equal respect and reciprocal consideration for everybody, is "universalistic" in the strict sense. Membership in this inclusive moral community, which as such is open to all, promises not only solidarity and a non-discriminatory inclusion, but at the same time the equal right of everybody to the protection of their individuality and otherness.

Discourses inspired by this idea are distinguished from all other discourses by two essential structural features. On the one hand, the universalistic discourses of law and morality can be misused for a particularly insidious form of legitimation, because particular interests can be hidden behind the gleaming façade of reasonable universality. As it happens, this ideological function, already denounced by the young Marx, is what underlies Carl Schmitt's resentment when he equates "humanity," the insistence on standards of egalitarian individualism, with "bestiality." What fascists like Schmitt seem to overlook, and what Marx clearly saw, is the other aspect of this discourse: the peculiar self-reference that first makes it into a vehicle for self-correcting learning processes. Just as every objection raised against the selective or one-sided application of universalistic standards must already presuppose these same standards, so too does any deconstructive unmasking of the ideologically obfuscating use of universalistic discourses actually presuppose the critical viewpoints advanced by these same discourses. Thus, moral and legal universalism is self-reflexively closed in the sense that one can criticize its imperfect practices only by invoking its own standards.

Question: One last question: what are your ideas on heroism?

J. H.: The courage, discipline, and selflessness demonstrated by the New York firemen who spontaneously put their lives on the line to save others on September 11 is

24

admirable. But why do we need to call them "heroes"? Perhaps this word has different connotations in American English than it does in German. It seems to me that whenever "heroes" are honored we must ask: who needs them and why? Even in this innocuous use of the term, one can understand Bertolt Brecht's warning: "Pity the land that needs heroes."

2
Interpreting the Fall of a Monument

On April 9, 2003 the entire world watched the scene in Baghdad as American troops threw a noose round the neck of the dictator and, surrounded by jubilant throngs of Iraqis, pulled him from his pedestal in a gesture charged with symbolic meaning. The apparently immovable monument swayed back and forth before falling. Before it crashed to the ground with a satisfying thud, there was a moment of suspension as the force of gravity sought to overcome the statue's grotesquely unnatural, horizontal posture. Bobbing gently up and down, the massive figure hung precariously in the air for one last horrible moment. And just as an optical illusion, looked at long enough, will undergo a gestalt switch, so the public perception of the war in Iraq seemed to perform a volte-face with this scene. The morally obscene infliction of shock and terror on a mercilessly bombarded, gaunt, and helpless population, morphed on this day in the Shiite district of Baghdad into the image of joyful citizens freed from terror and oppression. Both images contain an element of truth, even as they evoke contradictory moral feelings and attitudes. Must ambivalent feelings lead to contradictory judgments?

At first sight, the issue is simple enough. An illegal war remains a violation of international law, even if it leads to normatively desirable outcomes. But is this the whole story? Bad consequences can discredit good intentions. Can't good consequences generate a legitimating force of their own after the fact? The mass graves, the subterranean dungeons, and the testimony of the tortured all leave no doubt about the criminal nature of the regime. Moreover, the liberation of a brutalized population from a barbaric regime is a great good, indeed, the greatest of all political goods. In this regard, the Iraqis too, whether they are currently celebrating, looting, loitering apathetically, or demonstrating against their occupiers, are passing judgment on the moral nature of the war. Here in Germany, two reactions are emerging in the political public sphere.

On one side, the pragmatically minded believe in the normative force of the factual and rely on practical commonsense, which savors the fruits of victory with a keen sense for the political limits of morality. In their view, quibbling over the justification for war is simply *pointless* because it is now a historical fact. Others simply capitulate before the force of the factual, whether from conviction or opportunism. They brush aside what they now regard as the dogmatism of international law, on the grounds that this dogmatism, held captive by post-heroic squeamishness concerning the costs and risks of military force, has become blind to the true value of political freedom.

Both of these responses are inadequate. They both succumb to an emotional aversion to the supposed abstractions of a "bloodless moralism," without having grasped what the neoconservatives in Washington are actually offering as an alternative to the domestication of state power through international law. For the proposed alternative to the morality of international law is neither political realism nor the pathos of freedom, but a revolutionary vision: if the regime of international law fails, then the hegemonic imposition of a liberal global order is justified, even when it employs means that violate international law.

Wolfowitz is not Kissinger. He is a revolutionary, not a cynical technician of political power. To be sure, the

27

American superpower reserves the right to take unilateral and, if necessary, pre-emptive action and to employ all available military means to secure its hegemonic status against possible rivals. However, global power is not an end in itself for the new ideologues. What distinguishes the neoconservatives from the "realist" school of international relations is the vision of an American global political order that has definitively broken with the reformist program of UN human rights policy. Although this vision does not betray the liberal goals, it shatters the civilizing constraints which the UN Charter, with good reason, has placed on the means of realizing these goals.

*

To be sure, today the United Nations is not yet in a position to compel a non-compliant member state to guarantee democracy and the rule of law to its own citizens. And the highly selective enforcement of the UN's human rights policy is subject to the constraints of political realities: Russia need not fear an armed intervention in Chechnya because it is equipped with veto power. Saddam Hussein's use of nerve gas against his own Kurdish population is only one of many chapters in the disgraceful chronicle of failures of a community of states that averts its gaze even from genocide. All the more important, therefore, is the core mission of peacekeeping for which the UN was originally founded, that is, enforcing the prohibition against wars of aggression which, in the aftermath of World War II, led to the elimination of the *ius ad bellum* and set new restrictions on the sovereignty of individual states. With this, classical international law took at least a first decisive step along the road to a cosmopolitan rule of law.

For half a century, the United States could be counted on as the pacemaker for progress on this cosmopolitan path. However, with the war in Iraq, it has not only destroyed this reputation and abandoned its role as guarantor of international rights; its violation of international law sets a disastrous precedent for future superpowers. Make no mistake, the normative authority of the United States of America lies in ruins. Neither of the two conditions for a legally permissible deployment of military force was satisfied: the war was neither a case of self-defense against an actual or imminent attack, nor was it authorized by a decision of the Security Council in accordance with Chapter VII of the UN Charter. Neither Resolution 1441 nor any of the 17 previous (and "spent") resolutions on Iraq can be cited as a sufficient authorization. As it happens, the "coalition of the willing" confirmed this performatively by first seeking a "second" resolution, and declined to bring the motion to a vote only because it could not even count on the "moral" majority of the veto-less members of the Security Council. Ultimately, the whole procedure turned into a farce as the US President repeatedly declared his intention to act without a mandate from the UN if necessary. From the very beginning, the Bush Doctrine made it impossible to understand the military deployment in the Gulf region as a mere threat. For this would have presupposed that the threatened sanctions could have been *averted*.

Nor does a comparison with the intervention in Kosovo provide any mitigation. Granted, authorization by the Security Council was not forthcoming in this case either. But three circumstances of that intervention offered legitimation after the fact: first, the aim of preventing ethnic cleansing, which was known at the time to be taking place; second, the *erga omnes* provision in international law which mandates intervention to provide emergency aid in such cases; and, finally, the undisputed democratic and constitutional character of all the states participating in the vicarious military coalition. Today, by contrast, the normative disagreement is dividing the West itself.

Already at that time, in April 1999, a striking difference in strategies for justifying military action between the continental European and the Anglo-American powers

29

had become apparent. The Europeans had drawn the lesson from the Srebrenica disaster that armed intervention should be used to close the gap between effectiveness and legitimacy which had been opened by earlier peacekeeping operations, and thereby make progress toward a fully institutionalized cosmopolitan law. Conversely, England and America were content with the normative goal of promulgating their own liberal order internationally, if necessary with force. At the time of the intervention in Kosovo, I attributed this difference to contrasting traditions of legal thought – Kant's cosmopolitanism on the one side and John Stuart Mill's liberal nationalism on the other. However, in light of the hegemonic unilateralism which the architects of the Bush Doctrine have pursued since 1991,[1] one could conjecture in hindsight that the American delegation had already conducted the negotiations at Rambouillet from this original standpoint. Be that as it may, George W. Bush's decision to consult the Security Council was not motivated by any desire for legitimation through international law, for the latter had long since been dismissed internally as superfluous. Rather, this rearguard action was desired only to the extent that it broadened the basis for the "coalition of the willing" and soothed concerns among the American population.

Nevertheless, we should not interpret the neoconservative doctrine as an expression of normative cynicism. Geo-strategic objectives such as securing spheres of influence or access to essential resources, which such policy is also supposed to promote, may well invite analysis in terms of a critique of ideology. However, such conventional explanations trivialize what, until eighteen months ago, was still an unimaginable break with norms to which the United States had been committed. We would do well not to waste our time with speculations concerning motives but instead to take the doctrine at its word. To do otherwise would be to fail to grasp the revolutionary character of a political reorientation that draws its sustenance from the historical experiences of the last century.

*

Hobsbawm correctly described the twentieth century as the "American century." Neoconservatives can view themselves as "victors" and can adopt the undisputed American successes – the successful reordering of Europe and the Pacific and Southeast Asia after the defeat of Germany and Japan and the reorganization of Eastern and Central European societies after the collapse of the Soviet Union – as the template for a new world order to be realized under US leadership. From the perspective of a liberal *post-histoire* à la Fukuyama, this model has the advantage of making laborious and awkward discussions of normative goals pointless: what could possibly be better for people than the worldwide spread of liberal states and the globalization of free markets? Moreover, the road thereto is clearly marked: war and the arms race brought Germany, Japan, and Russia to their knees. In the current era of asymmetric warfare, military might is more attractive than ever, since the victor is determined a priori and can purchase victory with relatively few casualties. Wars that make the world better need no additional justification. From this point of view, wars remove undisputed evils that would continue to exist under the aegis of a powerless international community at the cost of collateral damage which can be disregarded. Saddam toppled from his pedestal *is* the argument – no further justification is required.

This doctrine was developed long before the terrorist attack on the Twin Towers. However, the cleverly manipulated mass psychology of the all-too-understandable shock of September 11 first created the climate in which the new doctrine could win widespread support, though in the rather different, heightened version of a "war against terrorism." This intensification into the "Bush Doctrine" results from defining an essentially new phenomenon in the familiar terms of conventional warfare. In the case of the Taliban regime, there was actually a causal connection between the elusive terrorism and a concrete "rogue state" that could become a target of attack. This provided a model for understanding classical interstate warfare as a means of defusing the insidious threat emanating from diffuse networks spanning the globe.

By contrast with the original version of the doctrine, this connection between hegemonic unilateralism and countering an insidious threat brings the argument for self-defense into play. But this also imposes new burdens of proof. The American government had to try to convince a global public that there had been contacts between Saddam Hussein and al-Qaeda. At least at home, the disinformation campaign was so successful that according to the most recent polls, 60 percent of Americans welcome the defeat of Saddam as "redress" for the terror attacks of September 11. However, aside from the difficulty of the lack of evidence, the Bush Doctrine does not really offer a plausible explanation for the *pre-emptive* use of military force. The violence of the new global terrorism – "war in peacetime" – escapes the categories of state warfare. It certainly cannot justify the relaxation of the strict clause regulating states' self-defense in international law to permit anticipatory *military* self-defense.

In the face of enemies who are globally networked, decentralized, and invisible, only prevention at *other* operative levels can be of help. Neither bombs nor missiles, neither fighter jets nor tanks, are of any help here. What *will* help is the international coordination of flows of information among national intelligence services and prosecutorial authorities, the control of flows of money, and, in general, the detection of logistics networks. The corresponding "security programs" in support of these goals concern civil rights within states, not international law. Other dangers arising from self-incurred policy failures concerning the non-proliferation of atomic, chemical, and biological weapons are in any case better handled through negotiations and inspections than through wars of disarmament, as the muted response to North Korea illustrates.

The intensification of the focus of the original doctrine onto terrorism, therefore, offers no gain in legitimacy for the direct pursuit of a hegemonic world order. Saddam toppled from his pedestal remains the argument: the symbol of a new liberal order for an entire region. The war in Iraq is a link in the chain of a new global political order that justifies itself as the replacement for the ineffectual human rights politics of an exhausted world organization. The USA becomes, so to speak, the trustee for the role in which the UN failed. What speaks against it? Moral feelings can lead us astray because they are tied to specific scenes and images. There is no way around the question of how to justify the war as such. The key disagreement is over whether justification through international law can and should be replaced by the unilateral, world-ordering politics of a self-appointed hegemon.

*

Empirical objections against the possibility of actually realizing the American vision converge on the thesis that global society has become far too complex to be controlled from a center through a politics backed by military power. In the fear driving the technologically heavily armed superpower, one can sense the "Cartesian anxiety" of a subject who tries to objectify both itself and the world around it in an effort to bring everything under control. Politics progressively loses ground to the horizontally networked media of both markets and social communication once it regresses to the original, Hobbesian form of a hierarchical security system. A state that reduces all of its options to the inane alternative between war and peace quickly runs up against the limits of its own organizational capacities and resources. It also diverts the process of political and cultural communication with competing powers and foreign cultures into false channels and drives the costs of coordination to dizzying heights.

However, even if hegemonic unilateralism could be implemented, it would generate *side effects* that are undesirable by its own normative criteria. The more political power (understood in its role as a global civilizing force) is exercised in the dimensions of the military, the intelligence services, and the police, the more it comes into conflict with its own purposes and endangers the mission of improving the world in accordance with liberal ideas. In the United States itself, the indefinite imposition of the program of a "wartime president" is already undermining the foundations of the rule of law. Quite apart from the methods of torture which are practiced or tolerated outside the nation's borders, the wartime regime is not only stripping the prisoners in Guantanamo of the rights they are entitled to according to the Geneva Convention; it is also expanding the powers of the security agencies in ways that infringe on the constitutional rights of American citizens. And wouldn't the Bush Doctrine demand normatively counter-productive measures if, as seems probable, were to make the citizens of Iraq, Syria, Jordan, Kuwait, etc., a less than friendly use of the very democratic freedoms which the American government wants to bestow on them? The Americans may have liberated Kuwait in 1991, but they did not democratize it.

Above all, however, the superpower's usurped role of trustee runs up against the objections of its own allies, who remain unconvinced *for good normative reasons* of its paternalistic claim to unilateral leadership. There was a time when liberal nationalism saw itself as justified in promulgating the universal values of its own liberal order, if need be with military force, throughout the entire world. Transferring this self-righteousness from the nation-state to a single hegemonic power does not make it any more tolerable. Precisely the universalistic core of democracy and human rights forbids their unilateral imposition at gunpoint. The universal validity claim which binds the West to its "basic political values," that is, to the procedure of democratic self-determination and the vocabulary of human rights, must not be confused with the imperialist claim that the political form of life and the culture of a particular democracy – even the oldest one – is exemplary for all societies.

The "universalism" of the ancient empires was of this sort. They perceived the world beyond the indistinct horizon of their frontiers from a perspective centered on their own worldview. The self-understanding of modernity, by contrast, has been shaped by an egalitarian universalism that requires a decentering of one's own perspective. It demands that one relativize one's own views to the interpretive perspectives of equally situated and equally entitled others. It was precisely American pragmatism that made insight into what is in each case equally good for all parties contingent on reciprocal perspective taking. The "reason" of modern rational natural law is not instantiated by universal "values" that one can own like goods, and distribute and export throughout the world. "Values" – including those that can count on winning global recognition – do not float in mid-air, but acquire binding force only within the normative orders and practices of particular cultural forms of life. When thousands of Shiites in Nasiriya demonstrate against both Saddam and the American occupation, they express the fact that non-Western cultures must appropriate the universalistic content of human rights with their own resources and in their own interpretation, one that establishes a convincing connection to local experiences and interests.

This is also why multilateral will-formation in interstate relations is not simply one option among others. From its self-imposed isolation, even the good hegemon, having appointed itself as the trustee of general interests, cannot *know* whether what it claims to do in the interest of others is, in fact, *equally* good for all. There is no coherent alternative to the progressive development of international law into a cosmopolitan order that ensures an equal and reciprocal hearing for the voices of all those affected. Thus far, the world organization has not suffered any really serious damage. It has even experienced an increase in esteem and influence because the "small" member states on the Security Council refused to buckle under the pressure from the larger states. The reputation of the world organization can suffer only at its own hand, by attempting, through compromises, to "heal" what cannot be healed.

II
The Voice of Europe in the Clamor of its Nations

3
February 15, or:
What Binds Europeans[1]

Preliminary remark: It is Jürgen Habermas's and my express wish to co-sign this analysis, which is at the same time an appeal. Setting aside the differences which may have divided us in the past, we regard it as both necessary and urgent that German and French philosophers should raise their voices together. As will be clear to the reader, Jürgen Habermas authored this text. Personal circumstances prevented me from writing a text of my own, though I would gladly have done so. I nevertheless agreed with Jürgen Habermas to co-sign this appeal whose premises and normative perspectives I substantially share: the definition of new European political responsibilities free from all Eurocentrism, the call for a renewed affirmation and effective reform of international law and its institutions, in particular, the United Nations, a new conception and new practice of distributing state powers, etc., in the spirit, and even the letter, of the Kantian tradition. Moreover, Jürgen Habermas's remarks overlap at many points with reflections that I recently developed in my book Voyous. Deux Essais sur la raison *(Galilée, 2002).[2] In a couple of days, a book by Jürgen Habermas and myself will appear in the United States with interviews that each of us gave in New York following September 11, 2001.[3] Notwithstanding the obvious differences in our approaches and modes of argumentation, this also reveals affinities between our views on the future of the institutions*

39

*of international law and the new tasks confronting Europe.
(Jacques Derrida)*

We should not forget two dates. The first is the day on which the newspapers reported to their flabbergasted readers the Spanish Prime Minister's invitation to the European governments willing to support the war in Iraq to swear an oath of loyalty to Bush behind the backs of their other EU colleagues. But just as little should we forget February 15, 2003, the day on which the masses of demonstrators in London, Rome, Madrid, Barcelona, Berlin, and Paris responded to this coup. The simultaneity of these overpowering demonstrations – the largest since the end of World War II – may go down in future history books as a signal for the birth of a European public.

During the leaden months leading up to the outbreak of the Iraq War a morally obscene division of labor had stirred up people's emotions. The large-scale logistical operation accompanying the inexorable military build-up and the hectic bustle of humanitarian aid organizations intermeshed like the wheels of a precision mechanism. The spectacle also unfolded dispassionately before the eyes of the population who were denied any independent initiative and who were destined to be its victims. No doubt about it, the power of emotions brought the united citizenry of Europe to its feet. At the same time, the war finally brought home to the Europeans the long-prefigured failure of their common foreign policy. As in the world as a whole, the casual violation of international law also sparked a controversy in Europe over the future of the international political order. However, the divisive arguments cut deeper here in Europe.

The well-known fault lines came all the more clearly to the fore in this dispute. The controversial stances on the role of the superpower, on the future world order, and on the relevance of international law and the UN brought the latent antagonisms into the open. The gulf between the continental and the Anglo-Saxon countries, on the one hand, and between "old Europe" and the Eastern European accession countries, on the other, became deeper. In Great Britain, the "special relationship" with the United States is by no means uncontroversial; but it continues to feature at the top of Downing Street's list of priorities. And although the Eastern European countries want to join the EU, they are not yet willing to restrict their sovereignty once again so soon after recovering it. The Iraq crisis was merely the catalyst. The constitutional convention in Brussels has also made manifest the conflict between those nations that really want to deepen the EU and those that have an *understandable* interest in freezing the existing mode of intergovernmental governance or, at most, making cosmetic changes to it. It is now no longer possible to paper over this conflict.

The future constitution will bring us a European foreign minister. But what use is a new office as long as the governments do not agree on a common policy? Even a Fischer with a new title would remain as powerless as Solana. For the present, only the core European member states are ready to endow the EU with certain features of a state. What should be done if only these countries can agree on a definition of "our interests"? If Europe is not to fall apart, these countries must now make use of the mechanism of "enhanced cooperation" agreed upon in Nice to take the initial steps toward a common foreign, security, and defense policy in a "Europe of different speeds." This will generate a momentum that the other members – initially those in the Eurozone – will not be able to resist in the long term. In the context of the future European constitution, there cannot and must not be any room for separatism. To take the lead does not mean to exclude. The core European avant-garde must not congeal into a Little Europe; it must play the role of a locomotive, as it has done so often in the past. The more closely cooperating member states of the EU will leave the door open to the others out of self-interest, if for no other reason. The invitees will be more willing to walk through this door the sooner core Europe also acquires the power to act in external affairs and shows that, in a complex world society, not only armies count but also the soft power of negotiation agendas, alliances, and economic benefits.

In this world, it does not pay to heighten politics into the alternative between war and peace, which is as obtuse as it is costly. Europe must throw its weight onto the scales at the international level and within the UN in order to counterbalance the hegemonic unilateralism of the United States. At global economic summits and in the institutions of the WTO, the World Bank, and the International Monetary Fund, it should bring its influence to bear in shaping the design of a future global domestic politics.

However, at present the policy of further expanding the EU is running up against the limits of the existing administrative steering mechanisms. Until now, the functional imperatives of creating a common economic and currency zone have propelled reforms. However, these driving forces are now exhausted. An *active* policy that calls not just for the removal of obstacles to competition but also for a common will on the part of the member states is dependent on the motives and convictions of the *citizens themselves*. Majority decisions on momentous new directions in foreign policy can only count on acceptance if the overruled minorities are in solidarity with the majority. However, that presupposes a feeling of political belonging. The peoples must "build," so to speak, a new European dimension onto their national identities. The already quite abstract civic solidarity which restricts itself to fellow-nationals must in future be extended to include European citizens of other nations.

This poses the question of "European identity." Only the consciousness of a common political fate and the convincing prospect of a common future can dissuade out-voted minorities from obstructing the majority will. The citizens of one nation must regard the citizens of another nation as "one of us" in principle. This requirement leads us to the question which inspires so many skeptical responses: are there historical experiences, traditions, and achievements capable of fostering among European citizens the sense of a shared political fate that they can *shape in common*? A compelling, let alone an inspiring, "vision" for a future Europe will not materialize out of thin air. Today only an unsettling sense of disorientation can induce it. However, the constraints of a situation in which we Europeans are thrown back upon our own resources *can* produce such a vision. Moreover, it must make itself heard in the wild cacophony of a clamorous public arena. If the topic has thus far not even found its way onto the agenda, then we have failed as intellectuals.

The Vagaries of a European Identity

It is easy to reach agreement on matters that do not involve serious commitments. We all share an image of a peaceful, cooperative Europe that is open to other cultures and is ready to engage in dialogue. We welcome the Europe which found exemplary solutions for two problems during the latter half of the twentieth century. The EU already represents a form of "government beyond the nation-state" that could serve as an example to be emulated in the postnational constellation. Moreover, the European social welfare systems counted for a long time as exemplary. Now they are on the defensive at the level of the nation-state. However, no future politics designed to tame capitalism in territorially unbounded spaces can afford to regress behind the standards of social justice which the welfare state established. If Europe met the challenge of two problems of this magnitude, why should it not also rise to the further challenge of defending and advancing a cosmopolitan global order based on international law against competing projects?

Of course, a pan-European discourse would have to meet with supportive dispositions that are waiting to be

43

activated, so to speak, by processes designed to promote self-understanding. Two facts seem to contradict this optimistic assumption. Haven't Europe's most important historical achievements lost their power to foster identity precisely because of their success throughout the world? Moreover, what is supposed to hold together a region that is marked like no other by the enduring rivalry between self-confident nations?

Because Christianity and capitalism, natural science and technology, Roman law and the Napoleonic Code, the bourgeois urban lifestyle, democracy and human rights, and the secularization of state and society have spread across other continents, these achievements are no longer the exclusive property of Europe. The Western mentality rooted in the Judeo-Christian heritage certainly has distinctive features. However, even this intellectual habitus, which is characterized by individualism, rationalism, and activism, is something that European nations share with the United States, Canada, and Australia. The "West," understood as a spiritual formation, comprises more than just Europe.

Moreover, Europe is made up of nation-states that set themselves apart from one another polemically. The national consciousness expressed in national languages, national literatures, and national histories has long represented an explosive force. However, the destructive power of nationalism gave rise to distinctive attitudes that lend contemporary Europe, with its incomparably rich cultural diversity, a characteristic profile in the eyes of non-Europeans. A culture that has over the centuries been torn apart more than any other by conflicts between city and country, ecclesiastical and secular power, the competition between religion and science, and the struggles between political authorities and antagonistic classes, had to learn the painful lessons of how differences can be communicated, oppositions institutionalized, and tensions stabilized. The recognition of differences, the mutual recognition of others in their otherness, can also become a distinguishing mark of a shared identity.

The pacification of class conflicts through the welfare state and the self-restriction of state sovereignty in the context of the EU are only the most recent examples of this. In the third quarter of the twentieth century, Europe west of the Iron Curtain experienced, in the words of Eric Hobsbawm, its "Golden Age." Since then, traits of a shared political mentality have become discernible, so that others often perceive us first as Europeans, rather than as Germans or French, and not just in Hong Kong but also in Tel-Aviv. It is true that secularization has advanced further, relatively speaking, in European societies. Here citizens tend to look askance at transgressions of the boundaries between politics and religion. Europeans have a relatively high level of confidence in the organizational accomplishments and steering capacities of the state, whereas they are skeptical of the effectiveness of the market. They have a sharp sense for the "dialectic of enlightenment" and do not harbor one-sidedly optimistic expectations concerning technological advances. They have preferences for the security guarantees of the welfare state and for regulations that strengthen social solidarity. The threshold of tolerance toward the exercise of violence against persons is relatively low. The desire for a multilateral and legally regulated international order goes along with the hope for an effective global domestic politics within the framework of a reformed United Nations.

The constellation which allowed the lucky Western Europeans to develop such a mentality in the shadow of the Cold War has collapsed since the events of 1989 and 1990. However, February 15 shows that the mentality itself has outlived the context which gave rise to it. That also explains why "old Europe" views the muscular hegemonic policies of its superpower *ally* as a challenge. And why so many in Europe welcome Saddam's fall as a liberation, while rejecting the illegality in international law of the unilateral, pre-emptive and inadequately and confusingly justified invasion. Yet, how stable is this mentality? Does it have roots in deeper historical experiences and traditions?

We now know that many political traditions that attempt to ground their authority in their naturalness were in fact "invented." By contrast, a European identity born in the public spotlight would have a frankly constructed character from the beginning. But only one based on *arbitrary* foundations would bear the taint of randomness. The ethical-political will instantiated in the hermeneutics of processes of self-understanding is not arbitrary. The distinction between the heritage we embrace and the heritage we wish to reject demands just as much consideration as the decision concerning the interpretation under which we appropriate it. Historical experiences are only *candidates* for the conscious appropriation without which they cannot exercise an identity-constituting force. In conclusion, I would like to offer some remarks on such "candidates" in light of which the contours of the post-war European mentality can emerge more clearly.

Historical Roots of a Political Profile

The relation between church and state in modern Europe assumed different forms either side of the Pyrenees, north and south of the Alps, and west and east of the Rhine. The religious neutrality of the state took on different legal forms in different European countries. However, within civil society, religion everywhere assumes a similarly apolitical role. Even if one may well regret this *social privatization of faith* in other respects, it has a desirable consequence for political culture. In Europe, a president who begins his official functions every day with a public prayer and connects his momentous political decisions with a divine mission is difficult to imagine.

46

The emancipation of civil society from the tutelage of absolutist regimes was not connected everywhere in Europe with the appropriation and democratic transformation of the modern administrative state. However, the impact of the ideas of the French Revolution across Europe explains, among other things, why here politics in both of its manifestations – as the medium for securing freedom and as organizational power – is regarded in a positive light. The imposition of capitalism, by contrast, was associated with pronounced class conflicts. This memory prevents an equally unequivocal assessment of the market. These contrasting valuations of *politics* and *the market* may also reinforce Europeans' confidence in the civilizing power of a state that they expect to compensate for "market failures."

The party system which emerged from the French Revolution has often been imitated. But only in Europe does it also serve to promote an ideological competition that exposes the pathological consequences of capitalist modernization within society to an ongoing political evaluation. This tends to promote *citizens' awareness of the paradoxes of progress*. Conservative, liberal, and socialist interpretations clash over the assessment of two aspects: do the losses generated by the disintegration of the protective traditional forms of life outweigh the gains of a chimerical progress? Or do the gains which current processes of creative destruction promise for the future outweigh the suffering of the losers in the process of modernization?

In Europe, the long-enduring impacts of class differences were experienced by those affected as a fate that only collective action could prevent. Thus, against the background of the labor movement and the traditions of Christian social thought, a solidary *ethos of struggle for greater social justice* aimed at universal welfare prevailed over an individualistic ethos of performance-based justice that accepts the inevitability of gross social inequalities.

47

Today Europe is marked by the experiences of the twentieth-century totalitarian regimes and by the Shoah, the persecution and destruction of the European Jews, in which the Nazi regime also ensnared the societies of the countries it conquered. The self-critical confrontations with this past have revived the memory of the moral foundations of politics. A heightened *sensitivity for violations of personal and bodily integrity* is reflected, among other things, in the fact that the Council of Europe and the EU have made the rejection of the death penalty a criterion of membership.

At one time in their belligerent past, all European nations were entangled in bloody conflicts. Their experiences of being mobilized against each other militarily and intellectually inspired them to develop new supranational forms of cooperation after World War II. The historical success of the European Union has confirmed Europeans in the conviction that the *domestication of the state's use of violence* also calls for a *reciprocal* restriction of the scope of sovereignty at the global level.

Each of the major European nations has experienced a flourishing of imperial power and, more importantly in the present context, has had to come to terms with the experience of the loss of an empire. For many countries, this *experience of decline* is associated with the loss of colonial possessions. With growing distance from imperial domination and colonial history, the European powers have also had the opportunity to *achieve a reflexive distance toward themselves*. In this way, they could learn to see themselves from the perspective of the defeated in the questionable role of victors who were called to account for the violence of an imposed and disruptive process of modernization. This may have contributed to the repudiation of Eurocentrism and have inspired the Kantian hope for a future global domestic politics.

48

4
Core Europe as Counterpower? Follow-up Questions[1]

Question: Reading your appeal in connection with your article "Interpreting the Fall of a Monument" (*Frankfurter Allgemeine Zeitung*, April 17, 2003),[2] one gets the impression that you are assuming that the role of the United States as the normative avant-garde of the twentieth century is finished and that you are proclaiming Europe as the new territorial and moral authority at the beginning of the twenty-first century. But if your proposal is to position Europe as the standard-bearer on the world stage, is there not a risk that playing up European peculiarities may have counterproductive consequences for the West, in general, and for the relation between Europe and the USA, in particular?

J. H.: The hegemonic vision which informs not just the rhetoric, but also the actions, of the current American government contradicts the liberal principles of the new world order which the father of the current President still advocated. If I may be permitted a biographical allusion: already as a schoolboy I was politically socialized entirely in the spirit of the ideals of the American and French eighteenth century. When I now assert that the moral authority which the USA derived from its role as an advocate of the global politics of human rights lies in shreds, then I am merely appealing to its own principles, as previously during the protests against the Vietnam

War. Our criticism measures itself against the better traditions of the United States itself. However, this will
become more than a melancholy lament only when Europe
recalls its own strengths.

Question: You distinguish seven identity-founding characteristics of Europe: secularization, the priority of the
state to the market, the primacy of social solidarity over
"merit," skepticism concerning technology, awareness of
the paradoxes of progress, rejection of the law of the
stronger, and the commitment to peace as a result of the
historical experience of loss. This conception of European
identity seems to rest primarily on a contrast with the US.
Isn't this opposition overstated given that they share universalistic orientations and given their shared opposition
to other images of political order – for example, that of
the fundamentalist religious state?

J. H.: Nobody needs to be told that there is a difference
in political mentality between Iran and Germany.
However, if the EU is to bring a competing project to bear
against the US in the elaboration of a universalistic international order, or if the EU is to offer at least a political
counterweight to hegemonic unilateralism, then Europe
must acquire self-confidence and an independent profile.
It must profile itself, not against "the" West, which we
ourselves are, nor against the liberal traditions of the
oldest democracy, which, after all, also have their roots
in Europe. It must take a stand against the dangerous
ideological politics of people who have come to power
under pretty contingent, not to say dubious, circumstances
and who will hopefully soon be elected out of office again.
We should not try to read a deeper meaning into these
contingencies by engaging in grand theorizing.

Question: Is the strong support for war in the US to be
traced back mainly to fundamental differences in mentality or rather to the influence of the media?

J. H.: When it comes to political suggestibility, we are all equally susceptible to the propaganda of Big Brother. The mobilization of the population and the exploitation of the all-too-understandable shock of September 11 by the conformist media may have something to do with the historical experiences of a nation that was spared until now; it is not a direct reflection of differences in mentality. I have traveled regularly to the US since 1965 and often remain there for a semester. My impression is that the room for open political debate has never been so constrained as it is at present. I would not have thought that this degree of official government opinion-formation and patriotic conformism would be possible, not in liberal America. However, the centrifugal forces acting on this multi-ethnic continent have never been so powerful either. And since 1989 there has not been an external enemy to perform the latent function of suppressing inner tensions. Many people in Washington will be happy that terrorism is taking over this role.

Question: You ascribe the central role in the future European unification process to a "core Europe." But who belongs to core Europe? Who should assume the driving role in the future as envisaged by the Nice mechanism?

J. H.: The "ongoing" project of conducting a symbolically effective and mentality-forming common foreign policy – which would be easy to institutionalize, by the way – must be undertaken by France, Germany, and the Benelux states. Then Italy and Spain would have to be won over. At present, it is not the populations but the governments that are the problem. The Greek government may well be open to a joint initiative.

Question: What role will Eastern Europe play in the future? Does the dividing line already run here between Europe and "the Rest" due to the lack of shared experiences over the past 50 years? Won't the Eastern

European accession states thereby be excluded in the long run?

J. H.: That's the obvious objection. But how can there be any question of "exclusion" when the door to accession is also wide open in this respect? I can understand the outlook of nations that want to enjoy their recently recovered sovereignty. I can also understand the conclusions concerning the Iraq War that a friend like Adam Michnik draws from the wonderful historical experience of the liberation from Soviet domination. But that's not the same thing as "exclusion." Here we must keep three facts in mind. First, the changing tempo of European unification has always been determined by the agreement between France and Germany to keep the process moving forward. For example, the whole process came to a standstill between Schröder and Jospin. Second, as the Eurozone demonstrates, there is already a Europe of different speeds. For the foreseeable future, Great Britain will not join the monetary union for its own reasons. Finally, the call for a common foreign policy is less an initiative than a reaction born of necessity. I can think of no better expression than the alternative posed by Richard Rorty: "Humiliation or solidarity."[3] The Eastern Europeans should not understand that as exclusion either, but as a call for solidarity with the rest of Europe.

Question: What significance does England have for Europe on your definition? Doesn't England lie closer to America than to Europe, in spite of the massive anti-war demonstrations, on account of its mentality, at least if one contrasts a Europe shaped by continental moral ideas with an Anglo-Saxon "utilitarian" space?

J. H.: The connection between philosophical traditions and the long-term orientation of national policies is not really that close. The emergence of the European Union always represented a problem for Great Britain – and it will remain so for the near future. However, Blair's loudly proclaimed advocacy for a unipolar world is just one position among many. As one can read in the liberal journal *Prospect*, the *special relationship* is by no means universally accepted in England. Moreover, unless I am mistaken, Blair's unconditional oath of loyalty to Bush rests on false premises – that will not escape people in England. If I may generalize, the English have a different conception of the future EU than have the Germans or the French. This difference exists independently of the Bush Doctrine and the Iraq War. In my opinion, Europe should not continue to brush this conflict under the carpet.

Question: In the past when you related your conception of constitutional patriotism to a shared history, it was always with an explicit warning against exclusivity and with a call for the inclusion of others. If we take the idea of a European constitutional patriotism as a model, wouldn't European identity have to be more strongly universalistic and more open?

J. H.: The idea that constitutional patriotism amounts to nothing more than the invocation of abstract principles is a tendentious misrepresentation of opponents who would prefer something palpably national. I can't resist the temptation to quote from a long interview I conducted with Jean Marc Ferry in 1988 on the concept of constitutional patriotism: "The same universalistic content must in each case be appropriated from out of one's own specific historical life-situation, and become anchored in one's own cultural form of life. Every collective identity, even a postnational one, is much more concrete than the ensemble of moral, legal, and political principles around which it crystallizes."[4] In the context of a pan-European political public sphere and culture, the citizens must develop a completely different political self-understanding than that expressed, for example, in American civil religion.

Question: To put the same question differently: doesn't this way of gearing identity to historically evolved collective mentalities run the risk of being understood substantively?

J. H.: On the contrary, the danger is rather that European commonalities have too little substance.

Question: What I mean is: what concrete European experiences are supposed to "found a sense of a shared political fate among European citizens that they can shape in common"?

J. H.: Well, we mostly learn from negative experiences. In my *Frankfurter Allgemeine Zeitung* article of May 31,[5] I recalled the religious wars, the conflicts between religions and classes, the decline of empires, the loss of colonial possessions, the destructive power of nationalism, the Holocaust – as well as the opportunities which can accompany the process of coming to terms with such experiences. The EU is itself an example for how the European nation-states have come to terms in a productive way with their belligerent past. If this project, which has now entered the phase of constitution-making, is successful, the EU could even serve as a model for forms of "government beyond the nation-state."

Question: Don't historical experiences within Europe differ markedly from each other, not just between "old" and "new" Europe, but also within each individual state?

J. H.: That's certainly true. Nevertheless, what separates them doesn't have to outweigh what is common, as it has until now. No one who has preserved a certain sense of history can imagine a Europe without Prague, Budapest, and Warsaw – no more than without Palermo. Historians have good grounds for describing Frederick II, who reigned in Sicily and Southern Italy, as the first "modern" monarch.

Question: What concrete meaning should we attach to your call that "the peoples must 'build,' so to speak, a new European dimension onto their national identities"?

J. H.: If the member states of a common currency zone are also to grow together politically, they will not be able to get by indefinitely without a harmonization of tax policy, and certainly not without harmonization of their various regimes of social policy. This is the toughest nut to crack because it calls for redistributions. Moreover, we won't be able to crack it as long as the Portuguese, Germans, Austrians, and Greeks are unwilling to recognize each other as citizens of the same political community. Even at the national level, the abstract, because exclusively legally mediated, solidarity among citizens is relatively thin. Nevertheless, in Germany this thin basis has been sufficient to sustain massive and continuing transfer payments from the West to the East even though they were separated for 40 years. In Europe, a much "thinner" solidarity will be sufficient; but this kind of civic sense of belonging together is nevertheless necessary. In this respect, the overwhelming demonstrations which took place simultaneously in London, Rome, Madrid, Berlin, Barcelona, and Paris on February 15 may represent the beginning of a trend.

Question: You postulate that Europe will foster a global domestic politics through international economic relations. But on what will these future European political initiatives be based if not on military efforts, as others have proposed?

J. H.: It won't be possible without any military efforts at all. The Iraq conflict has heightened awareness of the urgent need for a long-overdue reform of the United

Nations. The G8 summits have degenerated into empty rituals. I'm thinking primarily that even a global free trade policy needs direction and administration if it is not to produce asymmetrical advantages for one side and to ruin whole economies. The Eurozone states could pool their shares in the International Monetary Fund, the World Bank, and the Bank for International Settlements to bring their influence to bear on many questions, beginning with the organization of global financial markets, through trade disputes, to an adjustment of the parameters of tax policy. I am not an expert in this area, as you know. But it is not as if there is no alternative to the neoliberal rationality of the existing global economic regime, or even the interpretation of it defended in Washington.

Question: When you refer to the demonstrations of February 15 as the birth of a new European public sphere, you speak of London, Rome, Madrid, Barcelona, Berlin, and Paris. But weren't the protests, which extended from Jakarta to Washington, something more? Weren't they rather the manifesto of a new global public?

J. H.: I suspect that the reasons and motives for the protest in the West, on the one hand, and in the (Islamic) East, on the other, were not the same. Moreover, an intermittent global public – one occasionally centered around specific themes – has repeatedly emerged since the Vietnam War, interestingly mainly in response to wars or massacres. People seem to agree most readily across cultural boundaries in their spontaneous outrage over gross violations of human rights. However, not all horrors generate equal attention, as is shown by Rwanda and the Congo.

5
The State of
German–Polish Relations[1]

Question: German–Polish relations seem to be in a deep crisis. After 1989, there was much talk of a German–Polish community of interest. For over a year now we have been stumbling from one crisis to another: attitudes toward the United States and the Iraq War, the EU constitution, but also, yet again, history. How would you describe the current attitude of the Germans toward the Poles? What are the reasons for it?

J. H.: I cannot speak for "the Germans," of course. But as regards the Iraq War, the great majority of our population, as you know, took a clear stance against the warmongering of the administration in Washington. In my view, this was not only for pacifist reasons but also for far-sighted normative reasons. The reckless break with international law signals the superpower's intention to intervene as it sees fit in war zones. Whoever thrusts law aside in this way is shielding their own interests, values, and moral convictions from the demand for impartial justification in the relevant forums. Moreover, it gives other major powers a license to violate the prohibition on violence in an equally reckless manner when they see fit. As it happens, my generation acquired their faith in the civilizing power of international law from the Americans who founded the United Nations.

Certainly, many Poles find ample reasons for skepticism in their historical experiences concerning international treaties and organizations and the progressive constitutionalization of international law since 1945. However, the past is not always a good guide to the future. I'm especially surprised by the strange coalition between a weak, opportunistic post-communist government that is concerned for its reputation and the otherwise so principled intellectuals of the former opposition. This alliance played into the hands of a transparent American policy of division and it is now ready to let the European constitution fail with the acclamation of the nationalists. On the German side, the disappointment over the current developments plays a greater role than divergent historical memories in the increasing German–Polish tensions. On the Polish side, historical experiences are, understandably enough, once again feeding suspicions concerning German dominance in Europe. The German Reich conducted a total war on the Eastern front. The SS mobile killing units wreaked havoc in Polish towns and villages. The Nazis erected the death camps on Polish soil. We recruited forced labor in Poland and we murdered and abducted Poles.

Question: Germans have argued extensively over Nazi history – one need only think of the student movement and the Historians' Debate. Over the past two to three years, however, the emphasis of historical discourse seems to have shifted to German suffering during the Nazi period, to the aerial bombardment and the deportations. How do you view this change in German historical consciousness?

J. H.: Recall the first accounts of emigrants like Hannah Arendt and Max Horkheimer, who returned to the destroyed cities of their native country after World War II. At that time, the German population was suffused with self-pity for its own suffering. People saw themselves in the role of victims and for a long time forgot who the true victims were. This frame of mind, which Alexander and Margarita Mitscherlich analyzed as a form of repression, only began to change around the end of the 1950s. Since then we have experienced a series of waves: attempts to come to terms with the Nazi past and calls for the restoration of "normality" have succeeded each other. In the meantime, the Shoah has taken on the symbolic meaning of a warning throughout the world. The "politics of memory" – the attempts of later generations to come to terms with mass crimes and past complicity – has become normal in many countries, not only in Europe but also in South Africa, Argentina, and Chile.

By my estimate, however, the intensity of the controversies in Germany has not itself diminished, at least not in the media or in public discussion. Two things have changed with increasing historical distance. One concerns the routine exclusion and suppression which the established public sphere until now quite rightly exercised against opinions from the far right. Only through an informal but effective sanctioning wall between officially tolerated public speech, on the one hand, and privately expressed prejudices, on the other, could the political mentality of the population be successfully liberalized over the past decades. The mechanism functioned once again in the Hohmann affair.[2] However, three generations after Auschwitz, the political proscription of dangerous political attitudes must function even without an "artificial" gap between public and informal opinion designed to educate the public.

This challenge stands in a more or less arbitrary relation to the other phenomena you quite correctly describe. The Germans could not publicly mourn their own dead after the war. Their death was historically related to the deeds of a criminal regime that was supported by the mass of the population. Under these exceptional circumstances, we broke with the culture of memorials for the war dead rooted in the nineteenth century and are instead erecting a memorial for the murdered victims of the Germans. I supported this undertaking, but it was clear to me that this effort would leave traces. The desire to recuperate the public mourning for the war dead is not unnatural, though it is certainly also fraught with danger. This commemoration must not congeal into a collective narcissism and obdurately turn itself against others.

Question: What influence did the end of the Cold War and the unification of Germany have on the change in historical consciousness? Germany has become self-confident and self-assured.

J. H.: The populations of the two states grew farther apart than expected during the four decades of separation. The unification has led to mental antagonisms. In 1992 and 1993, homes for asylum seekers were burnt down[3] and an intellectual right, which had not existed until then, engaged in revisionism under the banner of the "self-confident nation." However, the danger of nationalistic derailment was banished on May 8, 1995 at the latest, when the mass of the German population retrospectively accepted the capitulation of May 8, 1945 as a "day of liberation" (contrary to the historical experiences of those living at the time). As it happens, I was in Warsaw on that day. I remember how difficult I found it to have to open a meeting on the fiftieth anniversary as a German in Poland, of all places.

Question: The sociologist Harald Welzer has made a study of National Socialism in the family memory of Germans. Contemporary Germans are indeed well informed concerning the horrors of the Nazi regime. However, the vast majority of them deny that their own relatives could have had anything to do with the Nazi crimes. Two-thirds of those questioned state that their parents and grandparents suffered greatly during the war. Only 1 percent of those

60

questioned do not rule out that their relatives were directly involved in the Nazi crimes. What implications does this have for historical consciousness?

J. H.: The 1968ers were reproached with being too mistrustful and self-righteous in their confrontations with their fathers. By that I don't mean to deny the prevalent tendency to rewrite one's own family history. Involvement in the crimes is foisted onto others, but at least onto other Germans. Perhaps this shifting of blame to nameless others is the price to be paid for a change in mentality in the younger generations.

Question: Isn't it dangerous when responsibility for the entire Nazi era is foisted onto a small Nazi clique? Won't future generations end up completely denying the responsibility of the German people as a whole for German history?

J. H.: I don't mean to justify distortion or repression in whatever form. But the psychological mechanism of splitting off one's family history from criminal occurrences in general does not necessarily lead to an interpretation of Nazi history that trivializes the broad acceptance of the regime, not to mention the crimes of the large mass of "willing helpers." In the more differentiated historiography and the endeavors at political enlightenment, the predominant tendency of the 1950s to make only a leading clique liable and to exonerate the people has been overcome. On the other hand, no one can predict how political mentalities will develop in Germany in the long term.

Question: In Poland people are very concerned about the idea of a Center against Expulsions initiated by Erica Steinbach of the League of Expellees and supported by many politicians and intellectuals.[4] Even intellectuals and public personalities like Leszek Kolakowski, Marek Edelmann, and Wladyslaw Bartoszewski are opposed to the idea. Are these Polish fears well founded?

J. H.: To be sure, the plan to erect such a center in Berlin is historically short-sighted, politically obtuse, and insensitive and, above all, not well thought-out. Many act as though the Eisenmann Memorial to the destruction of the European Jews in Berlin justifies the claim for some kind of "counterweight." However, this memorial documents precisely the break with the fatal ethnocentric tradition of the exclusionary commemoration of the victims of one's own nation. The serious problem of expulsions must be dealt with in its European dimensions and grasped in its full complexity. Then the claims of Wroclaw (Breslau) as a site for such a center are more urgent than those of Berlin.

I understand Polish fears of a revival of old mentalities in Germany. I myself shared them until the mid-1980s. But today I do not see any dramatic signs of a relapse. The Red-Green government may be more relaxed in its responses, but it is not ignorant of history. In this respect, the Poles could hardly wish for a more scrupulous Foreign Minister than Joschka Fischer.

Question: How do you see the problem of anti-Semitism in Germany? Is there a connection between anti-Semitism, anti-Zionism, and anti-Americanism?

J. H.: Yes, this ideological connection is typical of those forms of radical nationalism that played a major role in the collapse of the Weimar Republic. In Germany, anti-Americanism has always allied itself with the most reactionary currents and serves the most unregenerate elements as a cloak for anti-Semitism. On the other hand, fear concerning this historical complex clouds the current discussion and explains why the justified protest against the Iraq War and the well-founded criticism of the Sharon government are often met with misplaced suspicion. In Germany, there is still another factor at work. Many Jewish citizens could only gradually come to terms with living in the Federal Republic because they relied on the fact that in the final instance the United States would protect them. Thus, the polarization over the Iraq War has also led to a split in the liberal camp between Jewish and non-Jewish Germans. Therefore, we must preserve an even more clear awareness that anti-Semitism in the Federal Republic has a different significance from (the often even more pronounced) anti-Semitism in other countries.

Question: Then does Germany need a patriotism debate, a new definition of the concept?

J. H.: I regard this proposal of Frau Merkel, with all due respect, as nonsense. However, as the last direct witnesses die off, our ways of dealing with the monstrous aspects of our recent history must also change.

Question: You speak of constitutional patriotism. What does that mean in a European context?

J. H.: Even national consciousness did not materialize out of thin air. It established a fairly abstract form of solidarity among strangers. Poles are willing to make sacrifices for Poles and Germans for Germans, although they have never seen these other people in their lives. Civic solidarity that extends beyond local and dynastic boundaries is not natural, but first developed in the context of the nation-state. Now European unification is forcing us to overcome our national short-sightedness. The redistribution of burdens within a supranational community of 25 states cannot function properly without an extension of civic solidarity beyond national borders. The new accession countries are as much reliant on such transfer payments, if only for a limited period, as were formerly Ireland, Greece, and Portugal, for example.

Question: In Brussels, the heads of state did not manage to agree on a constitution for the EU. Perhaps the expanded Europe is too diverse and the fast German–French tandem is counterproductive when it comes to unifying the whole continent?

J. H.: The German government vigorously supported the membership of Poland and the other Eastern European countries. But the old member states failed on two counts in Nice. They were not able to agree on the goal of the European unification process as a whole. Should the unified Europe remain a glorified free trade zone, or shouldn't it also become an externally empowered political actor? They had no more success in deepening the institutions of the community in a sufficiently timely manner to ensure that a complex organism such as the enlarged Union is still governable. The constitutional convention came too late. Things were not helped by the Iraq War, which divided the European Union along an already longstanding, latent fault line. The American policy merely aggravated the opposition between the integrationists and their opponents. Historically speaking, one can easily understand Great Britain's *special relationship* with the US and Poland's need to defend its recently acquired national sovereignty from new restrictions. But then one should show equal consideration for the historical reasons underlying the desire of the Western European founding states that others should not prevent them from promoting a deeper integration. Among Germans, the hegemonic unilateralism of the United States reinforced the conviction that Europe must learn to speak with its own voice in the world. Only a complex, overlapping "Europe of different speeds" can lead us out of this dead end.

Question: You already pleaded in your article with Jacques Derrida for an avant-gardistic core Europe. Wouldn't that rather lead to the collapse of the EU?

J. H.: The scenario which has just unfolded in Brussels showed how a Europe that has become ungovernable could collapse under the pincer pressure of Great Britain, Spain, and Poland. Never before has the European Council allowed such an important project to fail in such an irresponsible manner. In addition, the absurd acting out of national egoisms has been followed immediately by the members' use of strong-arm tactics against each other in budgetary disputes. This fatal result was not conjured up by any plans for a core Europe but, rather, by the energetic attempt to make the Europe of the Twenty-Five march in step.

Question: Won't the alternative development of a core Europe pressing ahead with reforms entail a new division of the continent?

J. H.: If I understand you correctly, many Poles are torn between the fear of being oppressed by Germany and France, on the one hand, and being left behind by them, on the other. But with their progressive integration into a united Europe, these nations are also making themselves increasingly reliant on majority decisions. In order to render a core Europe credible as a transitional project that leaves the door open for all other members in its own interest, distributive decisions concerning the scope and use of the common budget must now be separated from constitutional political questions. Only when anger and mistrust diminish can it become apparent in practice that the fact that some countries take the lead does not necessarily mean that others are excluded. It must remain open to any member state to join in the favored forms of "enhanced corporation" at any time. The latter have long

65

since been provided for by the various European treaties and have already been partially realized by the completion of the monetary union. Besides, the whole image you invoke is misleading. A monolithic "core" would not develop if each of the partners agreed to cooperate more closely in specific areas, such as foreign policy, internal security, and tax harmonization.

6
Is the Development of a European Identity Necessary, and Is It Possible?

Following the failure of the European governments to agree on the draft constitution drawn up by the constitutional convention, the process of European unification has stalled once again. The mutual mistrust of the nations and member states seems to signal that European citizens lack any sense of mutual political belonging and that the member states are as far away as ever from pursuing a common project. Here I would like to address two questions: first, whether such a European identity is necessary (I) and, second, whether a corresponding transnational extension of civic solidarity is even possible (II).

In the course of the process of European unification, which has stretched out over almost half a century, intractable problems seem to have arisen repeatedly. In spite of this, the process of integration has progressed steadily even in the absence of recognizable solutions to these problems. This tends to confirm functionalists in their assumption that the political construction of a unified economic and monetary zone produces constraints whose intelligent processing *spontaneously* generates an increasingly dense network of transnational interdependencies in other social domains as well. The "path dependency" argument, according to which a decision procedure progressively constrains future alternatives, points to a similar conclusion. On this reading, political elites find themselves constrained, even against their will, to pursue an agenda that favors integration. For they are bound, due to unforeseen consequences, by the determinations of a set of decisions that were accepted in the past and have become progressively entrenched.

The thesis of a self-propelling process that inevitably leads to an "ever closer" union not only accounts for the policy of muddling through; it also relieves actors who have internalized this way of viewing things, and hence avoid addressing problems, of responsibility. Such interpretations enable elites to cling to the established mode of *intergovernmental* decision-making so that they do not need to concern themselves with a *normative* integration of citizens that would first make possible the pursuit of common goals across national boundaries.

Systemic integration and the entangling of elites in path-dependent decisions seem to render a common European consciousness superfluous. To the extent that social integration via values and norms is even necessary, it is supposed to arise spontaneously as a kind of by-product. I would like to show why the explanatory power of these social scientific hypotheses is now exhausted (1) and how the unification process is currently stalled before the threshold of a missing European identity (2).

(1) The problems we currently face are of a genuinely political nature and can no longer be settled solely by the functional imperatives of an indirect form of integration driven by common markets and the cumulative impacts of decisions. Three problems are now coming together: first, the immediate challenge of the eastern enlargement; second, the political impacts of the concluded process of economic integration, particularly for the Eurozone countries; and third, the altered global political situation.

First, the enlargement of the EU to the east by 10 additional states represents an increase in complexity that overtaxes existing structures and political steering procedures.[1] The capacity of the Union to govern cannot be assured even at the level of weak coordination without the adjustments called for by the draft constitution. Aside from the controversial question of the relative weights of votes, the subjection of additional fields of policy to majoritarian decision-making processes is especially relevant. Insofar as the principle of unanimity is abandoned, the intergovernmental style of negotiation which is the norm among international treaty partners must be replaced by the kind of procedure of deliberative decision-making which is familiar from our national arenas. However, that entails a major increase in the costs of legitimation. For minorities can only allow themselves to be outvoted when a relation of trust exists between them and the respective majorities. Only an awareness of shared membership can ground the feeling that one side is not taking advantage of the other.

Until now, the economic unification of Europe has not been a zero-sum game; everyone benefited from it in the medium term. Hence, the European populations, with few exceptions (Norway, Sweden), have accepted a unification policy imposed from above by elites. This kind of legitimation measured by "output" – that is, by results – can no longer insure acquiescence in policies that entail an unequal distribution of costs and benefits. For in such cases people want to have a say in advance and not just the possibility of punishing mistakes at election time. This problem will arise with increasing frequency following the eastern enlargement, because active political interventions will be necessary to bridge the gaps in socio-economic development between the old and new members. This will aggravate conflicts over the distribution of the scarce resources of a comparatively small EU budget, conflicts between net contributors and net beneficiaries, core and periphery, old recipients in Southern and new recipients in Eastern Europe, small and large member states, and so forth.

Second, active policies with distributive effects are not just a consequence of the accession of new member countries that exacerbate the existing differences in levels of economic development (for example, between Sweden and Portugal). Even in the Europe of the Fifteen, a need for coordination already arose that can no longer be met through the familiar mechanisms of a purely "negative integration" (Fritz Scharpf). As long as it was only a matter of institutionalizing equal market freedoms, *refraining* from doing something was sufficient to pressure governments into removing barriers to competition. By contrast, when the challenge is to harmonize fields of policy that have remained under national control, governments must actually *do* something. The construction of a unified economic and monetary zone creates a need for harmonization to which governments have responded initially since the EU summit in Lisbon with informal agreements.[2] These plans of action and methods of open coordination (peer review, benchmarking, policy learning) affect not only fields like the labor market and economic development, but also core domains of national policy such as immigration, the administration of justice, and criminal prosecution. Claus Offe even speaks of a "creeping Europeanization of social policy." This growing interconnection between national policies, in particular within the Eurozone, also calls for a democratic extension of the narrow basis of legitimation. A shifting of legitimation from the side of results to that of the co-determination of political programs that affect citizens of all member states equally, though not necessarily in the same ways, will not be possible without the development of an awareness of shared belonging to a political community that extends across national boundaries.

The third challenge comes from outside. Following the end of the bipolar global order, Europe is forced to redefine its role in the world and in particular its relation to the United States. Perhaps the modest efforts to form a common European security and defense policy exhibit most clearly the threshold before which the unification process has currently stalled. What is required is a form of pan-European democratic opinion- and will-formation that involves mutual observation of what is going on in the respective national arenas, even though it unfolds differently within each arena. Without this it will not be possible to have policies that can win the support of all of the member states of the Union in this symbolically charged area which is so crucial for integration.

(2)   The project of founding a constitution can be understood as an attempt to respond to these challenges. The new constitution is supposed to deepen integration, strengthen the capacity of the Union to make collective decisions, and reduce the widely lamented democratic deficit. The governments could even use the constitution itself as a vehicle for forming a European identity if they accepted an admittedly risky and unavoidably time-consuming change in their accustomed way of doing business, and if they involved the citizens themselves in the process of shaping the constitution through referenda. This is in any case advisable with such a project and is even more pressing because the debate concerning the new constitution has put the unsolved and suppressed problem of the "ultimate goal" [*Finalität*] of the unification process on the political agenda. This tricky question concerning the goal of the whole undertaking has two aspects. First, the question of the political structure of the Community: which Europe do we want? And, second, the question of geographical identity: what are the definitive boundaries of the European Union? The draft constitution leaves both of these questions open.

The question of which Europe we want cannot be given a satisfactory answer at the constitutional level alone, because the conventional concepts of state and international law are no longer valid. The dense web of supranational regulations emanating from Brussels and Luxemburg has long since invalidated the vision of a loose alliance of states as an adequate political framework for the common market and the common currency. On the other hand, the EU is equally far removed from the idea of a federal constitutional state of nationalities capable of harmonizing the financial and economic policies of the member states. The draft constitution implicitly recognizes the nation-states as sovereign subjects of treaties by leaving open an exit option. However, the delegates to the convention have worked out a "constitution" in the name of "the citizens *and* States of Europe." Thus Article I, Para. 1 begins with the Solomonic words: "Reflecting the will of the citizens and States of Europe to build a common future, this Constitution establishes the European Union. . . ." The convention accordingly gave its draft the title "*Treaty* Establishing a *Constitution* for Europe," and thereby sidestepped a conceptual opposition in terms of which international lawyers have thus far decided the question of sovereignty in favor of one side or the other. Viewed from a purely legal perspective, the priority of European over national law decides the question against the nation-states; but, politically speaking, things are not so simple.

On the other hand, the question of boundaries could have been dealt with in the constitution, of course. It was left open for political reasons. There seems to be a tacit agreement that the EU can expand further to the east only to include the remaining Baltic countries. All farther-reaching relations are supposed to be regulated by association agreements. Hence, the problem of where to draw the boundaries in effect boils down to the question of the accession of Turkey, which since Atatürk views itself as belonging to modern Europe. This question could be left open by referring to the relevant Copenhagen decision and the customary accession procedure.

Hence we must acknowledge that, as regards the question of its ultimate goal, the process of constitution formation is not producing any catalytic effect even though it is unfolding at a juncture when this latent inherited baggage has become increasingly burdensome. The question concerning the political structure and the boundaries of the future Union may have been touched upon within the convention, but this elite discourse behind closed doors has had no resonance beyond Brussels. Nor has it triggered any illuminating controversies concerning underlying attitudes, that is, the real motives behind the mute opposition between the pro-European and Euroskeptic camps. Everybody knows this but nobody is willing to say it out of fear of smashing the European family china. Berlusconi apart, the founding members of the Union count as more sympathetic to integration, whereas Great Britain, the Scandinavian countries, and the Eastern European accession countries (who are understandably proud of their recently recovered national independence) would prefer to preserve the intergovernmental format of the Union.

The conflict between integrationists and intergovernmentalists gets mediated in the daily activity of the expert commissions, but it is not conducted in the wider political public sphere as a dispute over goals and principles. In the controversies over the division of competences between the Union and the member states, on the one hand, and between the Parliament, the Council of Ministers, and the Commission, on the other, two main motives seem to be playing an important background role: historically rooted ideas concerning the current importance and role of the nation-state and the notions of order informing economic policy, in particular concerning the relation between politics and the market.

Those who continue to think in terms of classical foreign policy will tend to regard the nation-states as the primary international players. From this perspective, the EU represents just one international organization among others. To be sure, it features among the institutions and networks of the global economy as a force to be reckoned with; but it cannot and need not be entrusted with its

own *political mission*. On this view, the political will which
finds expression in the EU bodies is essentially directed
inwards. By contrast, those who conceive of the process
of economic globalization and the global political situation since September 11, 2001 as a challenge to develop
forms of "government beyond the nation-state," will see
the EU rather in the strategic role of a "global player."
Then it will seem natural to want to strengthen the collective capacity of Europe as a whole to take political
initiatives.

These conflicting perceptions of international developments are often associated with corresponding interpretations of the crisis of the welfare state. The Western
European countries confront the task of adapting their
tried and trusted social security systems to changed
demographic developments and changed global economic
boundary conditions. They are undertaking the overdue
renovation of the welfare state independently, each in its
own way; however, the underlying causes generating the
need for reform are not exclusively internal. It is not just
a matter of home-grown problems that fall within the
scope of national policy. Hence, we must pose the question of whether national governments only need to adapt
to altered boundary conditions, or whether they must also
exercise independent influence on the form that economic
globalization is taking via the global economic regulatory
institutions, if need be even in competition with the
United States. It is obvious that the governments which
are more sympathetic to interventionism than to neoliberalism can only invest their conceptions of a "European
social model" with substance with the help of an internationally empowered EU.

Conflicting perceptions of the constraints on diplomatic and military action in a destabilized global political
situation aggravate the polarization between these camps
even further. The policies of the present (and presumably
also the next) US government are guided by the image of
a unipolar world on which superpower hegemony alone

can avert the risks of fundamentalism (even one equipped with weapons of mass destruction) and impose political and economic modernization throughout the world. The European states have to choose between accepting the place within the framework of a "coalition of the willing" which Washington assigns its allies on this scenario and reinforcing the collective decision-making power of the EU with the aim of promoting a "reconstruction of the West"[3] under conditions of relative independence.

These background convictions polarize supporters and opponents of a deeper integration right across all nations. However, the unbalanced spectrum of opinion among the various nations also drives the actions of the governments of the larger member states in opposing directions. When Churchill urged France and Germany to take the lead in unifying Europe in his famous University of Zurich address of 1946, he saw Great Britain quite naturally as standing alongside the US and Russia as well-wishers and facilitators, but not as participants in the project. At times, Margaret Thatcher and Tony Blair give the impression that nothing much has changed since then in this historical perception of the natural order of things. Other historical forces underlie Euroskepticism in other countries. Following the failure of the constitution, at least for the time being, and the immediately ensuing conflict over the increase in the EU budget, a European Union torn apart by internal conflicts is looking increasingly like a new platform for the old game of the European powers. An EU directorate composed of France, Great Britain, and Germany would not, after all, assume the role of a core European pacemaker, but would be subject to the temptation to regress to the familiar balance of power politics between mutually jealous nation-states under the transformed conditions of intergovernmentalism.[4]

This lamentable condition in which the European Union finds itself seems to confirm the "no demos thesis" that a European constitution is not possible because a constitution founding "subject" does not exist. According to this thesis, the Union will not be able to develop into a political community with its own identity "because there is no European people." This argument is based on the assumption that only a nation united by a shared language, tradition, and history can provide the necessary basis for a political community. For only on the basis of shared ideals and values are members willing and able to accept reciprocal rights and duties and can they have confidence that observance of these norms will be fair to all sides. I would like to show that this interpretation will not withstand closer examination, even though the history of the European nation-state initially seems to support it (1). Granted, the question of whether something like a European identity exists must be answered in the negative for the present. However, this is the wrong question. The real issue concerns the conditions that must be fulfilled if the citizens are to be able to extend their civic solidarity beyond their respective national borders with the goal of achieving mutual inclusion (2).

(1) An abstract, legally mediated solidarity among citizens first arose within the context of the European nation-state. This new political form of solidarity among strangers only emerged in tandem with the equally novel national consciousness. The process by which the local, dynastic bonds among compatriots to religiously grounded political authority were extended into a political consciousness of active membership in a democratically constituted nation is an example of the communicative dissolution of traditional duties and loyalties. For national consciousness is a thoroughly modern form of consciousness, though it assumes a pseudo-natural appearance. The idea of national history was an academic construct made possible by historians, folklorists, linguists, and literary critics. It was

introduced into the educational process via the school and family, disseminated through mass communication, and anchored in the outlook of generations primed for war through the mobilization of conscripts.

It generally took almost a century before this process had pervaded the whole population. Clearly, egalitarian commitment to universalistic principles of constitutional democracy also developed only on the basis of this ethno-nationally extended particularism. However, the fusion of these two elements – nationalism and republicanism – in the nation-state has loosened following two world wars and the excesses of radical nationalism, and not just in Germany. Thus, when we consider the question of a possible extension of national solidarity we must take into account the transformations of civic solidarity which have occurred in the interim.

Republican convictions float free from their pre-political moorings only insofar as democratic practices develop an *internal dynamic* of public processes of political self-reflection. That such an identity-shaping internal dynamic of public discourse is possible is shown by the fact that conflicts of interest sparked, for example, by health-care reform, immigration policy, or questions relating to the Iraq War and compulsory military service are nowadays addressed in light of principles of justice rather than in terms of the "fate of the nation." Competition for jobs and investment is, after all, a different matter from the nation's struggle for "Lebensraum" or a "place in the sun." Civic solidarity is in any case paid for only in small change: income tax replaces the heroic duty to sacrifice one's life for one's country. We are no longer ready to die for Berlin or Paris, any more than we are for Nice. (Hence, even the Anglo-Saxon countries could not have conducted the Iraq War under conditions of general conscription.)

The self-critical "politics of memory," which has in the meantime spread far beyond Germany, exemplifies how constitutional patriotic bonds can develop and be renewed *in the medium of politics itself.* The political controversies

77

surrounding the commemoration of the Holocaust and the mass crimes of the Nazi regime in general have led German citizens to understand their constitution as an achievement. Citizens do not internalize constitutional norms in an abstract form but concretely, in the context of their respective national histories. As a component of a liberal culture, these principles must become woven into the dense web of historical experiences and pre-political values.

An important shift in emphasis occurs in the course of this transition to a postnational form of consciousness – the peculiar switch in emotional fixation from the state to the constitution. Whereas *national consciousness* crystallized around a form of state in which the people could recognize themselves as a collectively empowered actor, *civic solidarity* grows out of membership in a democratically constituted political community of free and equal citizens. In the foreground is no longer the self-assertion of the collective toward the outside, but the preservation of a liberal order within. To the extent that *identification with the state* mutates into an *orientation to the constitution*, the universalistic constitutional norms acquire a kind of priority over the specific background context of the respective national histories.

This switch from a fixation on the state to an orientation to the constitution enables the structure of a "solidarity among strangers" that is inherently abstract and mediated by law to emerge already within the context of the nation-state. Moreover, this structure clearly meets a transnational extension of national solidarity halfway. The more attention is focused on the same universalistic content beyond national boundaries, the less controversial become the legal norms which have long since determined the construction of supranational organizations and the adjudication of international courts. One aspect of this is particularly interesting: the more constitutional patriotic commitments outweigh the fixation on the state, the greater becomes the affinity for a development currently discernible at the supranational level, namely, toward a gradual "uncoupling of the constitution from the state."[5]

(2)   Whereas constitutions found an association among legal subjects, states organize practical capacities. Viewed historically, nation-states arose from revolutionary situations in which citizens compelled repressive states to grant them their liberties. Postnational constitutions lack this pathos, for they arise from a completely different situation. Today states, which have long since constituted themselves as constitutional democracies, find themselves exposed to the risks of an increasingly interdependent global economy. They are responding to this challenge by creating supranational orders that go beyond merely coordinating the activities of individual states.[6] International associations and organizations assume the form of constitutions or functionally equivalent treaty complexes without already thereby acquiring the character of the state. These constituted political communities are outrunning, so to speak, the construction of supranational practical capacities. A relative uncoupling of the constitution from the state is shown, for example, by the fact that supranational communities such as the UN or the EU do not possess the kind of monopoly on the means of legitimate violence which served as a reserve for the sovereignty of the modern administrative, legal, and tax-based state. In spite of the fact that nation-states enjoy a decentralized control over the means of violence, the European law passed in Brussels and Luxemburg, for example, enjoys priority over national law and is applied in the member states without objection, so that Dieter Grimm can assert that the EU treaties already amount to a "constitution."

As regards the question of a possible extension of civic solidarity beyond national boundaries, we must indeed take into account the characteristic differences between the UN and the EU. A narrow basis of legitimation is sufficient for a functioning world organization that includes all states and rejects social boundaries between "ins" and "outs" as long as it restricts itself to the functions of human rights policy and peacekeeping. Shared moral outrage over gross transgressions of the prohibition on violence and egregious violations of human rights provides a sufficient basis for solidarity among world citizens. At present, we can already observe the beginnings of the communicative structures of the global public sphere which this requires; even the outlines of the cultural dispositions required for a worldwide harmonization of moral reactions are already discernible. In other words, the functional requirement that cosmopolitan society should be weakly integrated through negative emotional reactions to perceived acts of mass criminality (prosecuted by the International Criminal Court) should not represent an insuperable hurdle.

However, this potential is not sufficient to integrate a European Union that, we would like to assume, learns to speak with one voice in foreign policy and acquires the necessary competences to conduct an active domestic policy. Solidarity among the citizens of a political community, no matter how large and heterogeneous, cannot be produced *solely* through the strong negative duties of a universalistic morality of justice (which, in the case of the UN, means the duty to refrain from wars of aggression and egregious violations of human rights). Citizens who recognize each other as members of a particular political community act, rather, with an awareness that "their" community differs from others by a collectively privileged and tacitly accepted form of life. Such a political ethos is no longer something natural. As the result of the formation of a political self-understanding which always accompanies the democratic process, it arises in a transparent fashion and it is clear to all concerned that it is a construct.

The national consciousness which already arose in the nineteenth century was such a construct, though not yet for the citizens themselves. Thus the question is not whether a European identity "exists," but whether the national arenas can be so opened up to each other that a self-propelling process of shared political opinion- and will-formation on European issues can develop above the national level. Today a European political self-understanding can only develop on the basis of democratic processes and, it goes without saying, through a non-pejorative differentiation from the citizens of other continents.

The structure of civic solidarity does not pose an obstacle to this envisaged extension beyond national boundaries. However, increasing trust is not only a *result* but also a *presupposition* of a shared process of political opinion- and will-formation. Until now, the process of European unification has taken such a circular form. Today, too, the path to a democratic deepening of the Union and to the requisite mutual networking of national public spheres can only proceed via such an *already accumulated* capital of trust. In this regard, it is impossible to overestimate the importance of the reconciliation between France and Germany.

The divisive force of divergent national histories and historical experiences that traverse European territory like geological fault lines remains potent. The earthquake unleashed by the illegal Iraq policy of the Bush administration has also torn our countries apart along these historical fault lines. The potential stored up in national memory has a particular explosive power because the nation-states are also the "sovereign subjects of the European treaties." Other conflicts (such as those between major regions, social classes, religious communities, alliances of political parties, and groups of accession countries, or between the size and economic weight of member states) concern interests that intersect and overlap transnationally in such a way that they may have a unifying, rather than a divisive, effect for the European Union.

If such historically rooted conflicts are indeed again hindering the process of European unification, then the concept of "different speeds" acquires renewed relevance. Before launching, like the German foreign minister, into flights of fantasy over the wide-ranging strategic tasks of the enlarged European Union in the world,[7] the political elites should reflect on the limitations of a bureaucratic mode of administration. They first need to pose the question of how and where the controversial goal of European unification can become the focus of an effective process of political communication among the citizens themselves. A political civic identity, without which Europe cannot acquire the capacity to act independently, can only evolve within a transnational public space. This process of consciousness formation cannot be controlled from above by elites nor, unlike the exchange of goods and capital in the common economic and currency zone, can it be "produced" by administrative decisions.

III
Views on a Chaotic World

7
An Interview on
War and Peace[1]

Question: You were also very critical of the American-led war in Afghanistan and Iraq. But during the Kosovo crisis you supported similar unilateralist action and defended a form of "military humanism," to use Chomsky's expression. How do these cases differ – Iraq and Afghanistan on the one hand, and Kosovo on the other?

J. H.: I expressed myself with some reservation concerning the intervention in Afghanistan in the interview with Giovanna Borradori: after September 11, the Taliban regime refused to renounce unambiguously its support for the terrorism of al-Qaeda.[2] Until now, international law has not been designed for such situations. The objections I had at the time were not, as with the Iraqi campaign, of a legal nature. Quite apart from the mendacious tactics of the current US government which have subsequently come to light, the recent Gulf War represented an open break with international law, indeed one with which Bush publicly threatened the United Nations from September 2002 onwards. Neither of the two preconditions which could have justified such an intervention was fulfilled: there was neither a relevant resolution of the Security Council nor was an attack by Iraq imminent. The issue of whether weapons of mass destruction would be found in Iraq or not was beside the point. There can be no retroactive justification for a preventive attack: no one may go to war on a suspicion.

Here you see the difference from the situation in Kosovo, when the West had to decide in light of the experiences of the Bosnian War – think of the disaster of Srebrenica! – whether it wanted to stand by while Milosevic conducted yet more ethnic cleansing, or whether it wanted to intervene even in the absence of clear national interests. Admittedly, the Security Council was deadlocked. Nevertheless, there were two legitimating reasons, one formal, the other informal, even though they are no substitute for the consent of the Security Council which is mandated by the UN Charter. First, one could appeal to the *erga omnes* obligation, binding on all states, to provide emergency assistance in the case of an impending genocide, which is at any rate an established part of international law. Second, one can point to the fact that NATO is an alliance of liberal states whose internal constitutions conform with the principles of the UN Declaration on Human Rights. Compare this with the "coalition of the willing" which split the West and included states that systematically violate human rights, such as Uzbekistan and Taylor's Liberia.

Equally important is the perspective from which the continental European countries like France, Italy, and Germany defended their participation in the Kosovo intervention at the time. In the expectation that the Security Council would later endorse their undertaking, these countries understood this intervention as an "anticipation" of an effective cosmopolitan law, that is, as a step on the path from classical international law to what Kant envisioned as a "cosmopolitan condition" that would grant citizens legal protection even against their own criminal governments. Already at that time (in an article for the April 29, 1999 issue of *Die Zeit*), I identified a characteristic difference between the continental Europeans and the Anglo-Americans: "It is one thing for the United

States to instrumentalize human rights by playing the role of hegemonic guarantor of global order in accordance with its political traditions, however admirable these may be. It is quite another for us to understand the precarious transition from classical power politics to a cosmopolitan order as a learning process to be mastered collectively. This more comprehensive perspective also calls for greater caution. The self-empowerment of NATO should not become the rule."[3]

Question: On May 31, you and Derrida published a manifesto of sorts under the title: "February 15, or: What Binds Europeans. A Plea for a Common Foreign Policy – Beginning with Core Europe." In a preliminary remark, Derrida explains that he is co-signing the article which you wrote.[4] How is it that two intellectual heavyweights who for the past two decades have eyed each other suspiciously across the Rhine – while, as some maintain, talking past each other – could suddenly agree to co-publish such an important document? Is it simply "politics," or is the text you co-signed also a "philosophical gesture"? An amnesty, a truce, a reconciliation, a philosophical gift?

J. H.: I have no idea how Derrida would answer your question. For my taste, your formulations smack of overstatement. First, it is, of course, a political statement, one on which Derrida and I happen to agree – as has often occurred in recent years, by the way. After the formal conclusion of the Iraq War, when many people feared a general prostration of the "unwilling" governments before Bush, I sent a letter to Derrida – as well as to Eco, Muschg, Rorty, Savater, and Vattimo – inviting them to participate in a joint initiative. (Paul Ricoeur was the only one who declined for political reasons; Eric Hobsbawm and Harry Mulisch could not participate for personal reasons.) Derrida, too, was not able to write an article of his own because he had to undergo unpleasant medical tests at the time. However, Derrida very much wanted to be part of the initiative and suggested the procedure which we then followed. I was happy about this. We had last met in New York after September 11. We had already resumed our philosophical conversation some years previously in Evanston, Paris, and Frankfurt. So there was no need for a grand gesture.

Derrida, for his part, gave a very subtle lecture in the Paulskirche in Frankfurt on receiving the Adorno Prize, which revealed the intellectual affinity between these two thinkers in an impressive way. Such a gesture does not leave one unmoved. Moreover, aside from all political questions, what unites me with Derrida is the philosophical reference to an author like Kant. Admittedly, we part ways over the later Heidegger – even though we are roughly the same age, our life histories have been very different. Derrida assimilates Heidegger's ideas from the Jewish-inspired standpoint of a Levinas. I encounter Heidegger as a philosopher who failed as a citizen, in 1933 and especially after 1945. But he is suspect for me even as a philosopher because, during the 1930s, he interpreted Nietzsche precisely in the neo-pagan fashion then in vogue. Unlike Derrida, whose reading of "*Andenken*" (lit. "remembrance") accords with the spirit of monotheistic tradition, I regard Heidegger's botched "*Seinsdenken*" (lit. "thinking of being") as a leveling of the epochal threshold in the history of consciousness which Jaspers called the "Axial Age." On my understanding, Heidegger betrayed that caesura which is marked, in different ways, by the prophetic awakening of Mount Sinai and by the enlightenment of a Socrates.

Insofar as Derrida and I understand each other's respective background motives, then the fact that we differ over an interpretation need not mean that we differ over the thing interpreted. At any rate, "truce" and "reconciliation" are not the right terms for a congenial, open-minded exchange.

88

Question: Why did you give this essay the title "February 15" and not, as some Americans would suggest, "September 11" or "April 9"?[5] Was February 15 the world-historical response to September 11, rather than to the campaigns against the Taliban and Saddam Hussein?

J. H.: You are reading too much into it. By the way, the editors at the *Frankfurter Allgemeine Zeitung* published the article under the headline "Our Renewal. After the War: The Rebirth of Europe." Maybe they wanted to downplay the importance of the demonstrations of February 15. By alluding to this date, I wanted to emphasize that the largest demonstrations since the end of World War II had taken place in cities like London, Madrid, Barcelona, Rome, Berlin, and Paris. These demonstrations were not an answer to the attack of September 11, which immediately inspired impressive displays of solidarity among Europeans. Rather, the demonstrations gave voice to the impotent, infuriated outrage of a highly diverse mass of citizens, many of whom had never before taken to the streets. The anti-war appeal was directed unambiguously against the mendacious and illegal policies of certain of the allied governments. I regard this mass protest as no more "anti-American" than our Vietnam protests were in their day, with the regrettable difference that, between 1965 and 1970, we only had to add our voices to the dramatic protests then occurring in America itself. So I was glad that my friend Richard Rorty spontaneously joined in our initiative of May 31 with an article that was, as it happens, politically and theoretically the most astute.

Question: Let's stay with the original title, which called for a common European foreign policy "beginning with core Europe." This implies that there's a center and a periphery, that some countries are indispensable and others not. To some ears, this sounded like an eerie echo of Rumsfeld's distinction between "old" and "new" Europe. I'm sure that the ascription of any such family resemblance gives you and Derrida a headache. You have been a vocal advocate of a constitution for the European Union in which such gradations of space and geography have no place. What do you mean by "core Europe"?

J. H.: "Core Europe" is in the first place a technical expression given currency at the beginning of the 1990s by the foreign policy experts of the CDU, Wolfgang Schäuble and Karl Lamers, at a time when the process of European unification had stalled once again. It was supposed to recall the vanguard role played by the six original members of the European Community. Then as now, the idea was to underscore the role played by France, the Benelux countries, Italy, and Germany as the driving force behind the "deepening" of the EU institutions. In the meantime, a provision for an "enhanced cooperation" among individual member states in particular fields of policy was even officially adopted at the Nice summit of EU heads of government. This mechanism now appears in the draft European Constitution under the heading of "structured cooperation." Germany, France, Luxemburg, Belgium, and recently even Great Britain, are making use of this provision to develop a joint European military force. However, the US administration is exercising considerable pressure on Great Britain to forestall the creation of a European military force that would only have an associative relationship with NATO. To this extent, therefore, "core Europe" is already a reality.

On the other hand, of course, the term has now acquired a provocative connotation in a Europe deliberately split and weakened by Rumsfeld and his cronies. The idea of a common foreign and defense policy issuing from a core Europe arouses anxieties at a time when the European Union is barely governable following eastern enlargement. This is particularly true for those countries that resist further integration for understandable historical reasons. Some member states want to preserve their national freedom of action. They are more interested in maintaining the existing, largely intergovernmental mode of decision-making than in extending the jurisdiction of supranational institutions with majoritarian decision-making procedures to a progressively larger number of policy fields. Thus, the new Eastern European accession countries are concerned about their newly acquired national sovereignty and Great Britain is afraid of losing its "special relationship" with the USA.

America's policy of splitting the Europeans found willing helpers in Aznar and Blair. Their chutzpah met with the long-latent fault line dividing the integrationists from their opponents. "Core Europe" is an answer to both – to the smoldering internal European conflict over the "ultimate goal" [*Finalität*] of the unification process, which is completely independent of the war in Iraq, and to the current fomenting of that conflict from outside. The reactions to the catch phrase "core Europe" become even more nervous the more external and internal pressures invite this answer. The hegemonic unilateralism of the US administration has issued a challenge to Europe to learn, finally, to speak with one voice in foreign policy. However, in view of the stalled process of deepening the European Union, we can only learn to do that if we first make a beginning at the center.

Over the decades, France and Germany have often assumed this role. Taking the lead does not mean excluding. The doors remain open for everyone. The harsh criticisms leveled at our initiative, especially from Great Britain and Eastern Europe, are also explained, of course, by the aggravating circumstance that the push for a common foreign and defense policy in core Europe came at a moment when the overwhelming majority of the population throughout Europe had rejected participation in Bush's Iraq adventure. For me, this provocative aspect of our May 31 initiative was welcome. Regrettably, though, it did not lead to a fruitful discussion.

Question: We know, of course, that the United States also used its influence within NATO to play off "new" Europe against "old" Europe. Will the future of the European Union bring a weakening or a strengthening of NATO? Can and should NATO be replaced by something else?

J. H.: NATO played a positive role during the Cold War and afterwards as well, though there should not be a repeat of the unilateralism of the Kosovo intervention. However, NATO has no future if the United States increasingly sees it less as an alliance involving obligations to consult and more as an instrument for promoting its unilateral national interests and superpower politics. NATO's peculiar strength lies in the fact that its significance is not limited to its function as a powerful military alliance but that it unites military combat capability with a value-added *dual legitimacy*. NATO's existence is justified, in my view, only as an alliance of unquestionably liberal states that expressly acts in strict conformity with the human rights policies of the United Nations.

Question: "Americans are from Mars; Europeans are from Venus," writes Robert Kagan in an essay that has attracted considerable attention from the neoconservative Straussians in the Bush administration. One could even view this essay, which was originally entitled "Power and Weakness," as the manifesto from which Bush developed the national security doctrine.[6] Kagan distinguishes between Americans and Europeans, calling the former "Hobbesians" and the latter "Kantians." Have the Europeans really entered the postmodern paradise of Kant's "perpetual peace," while the Americans remain outside in the Hobbesian world of power politics, guarding the ramparts which their European beneficiaries are incapable of defending?

J. H.: The philosophical comparison won't get you very far. Kant himself was, in a certain sense, a loyal student

92

of Hobbes; at any rate, his description of modern coercive law and of the nature of state power is as sober as that of Hobbes. Kagan's over-hasty and simplistic connection between these philosophical traditions, on the one hand, and national mentalities and policies, on the other, is best overlooked. The differences in mentalities which one can discern between Anglo-Americans and continental Europeans when viewed from a great distance reflect long-term historical experiences; but I see no correlation with short-term shifts in political strategies.

However, in his effort to separate the wolves from the sheep, Kagan points to a number of facts: it took military force and, ultimately, the intervention of the United States to bring down the terror regime of the Nazis. During the Cold War, the Europeans were only able to build and extend their welfare states behind the nuclear shield provided by the United States. Pacifist attitudes have taken root in Europe, especially in its densely populated center. For the present, European countries, with their comparatively slender military budgets and poorly equipped armed forces, have nothing with which to oppose the crushing military might of the US except empty words. Nevertheless, Kagan's caricatured interpretation of these facts invites a number of responses:

- we also have the campaigns of the Red Army, which were so costly in lives, to thank for the victory over Nazi Germany;
- Europeans' social compact and economic weight are features of a "soft," non-militaristic power that insure their considerable influence in the global balance of power;
- in Germany today, a welcome pacifism – in part, a product of American re-education – prevails, though it did not prevent the Bundesrepublik from participating in UN missions in Bosnia, Kosovo, Macedonia, Afghanistan and most recently in the Horn of Africa;

93

- the US itself is thwarting the plans to build a European military capability independent of NATO.

This exchange of blows elevates the matter to the false level of a controversy. What is completely false, in my view, is Kagan's stylization of US policy over the course of the last century. The struggle between "realism" and "idealism" in foreign and defense policy was not played out between the continents but within American politics itself. To be sure, the bipolar global power structure between 1945 and 1989 necessitated a policy of balance of terror. During the Cold War, the competition between the two nuclear powers provided the backdrop for the overwhelming influence of the "realist" school of international relations in Washington. However, this should not lead us to forget the impetus President Wilson gave to the founding of the League of Nations after World War I, nor the influence wielded by American jurists and politicians in Paris even after the US government withdrew from the League. Without the US, the Kellogg-Briand Pact, and hence the first international legal proscription of wars of aggression, would never have come about. Above all, the policy of the victors in 1945, initiated by Franklin D. Roosevelt, is difficult to reconcile with the militant picture of the role of the US painted by Kagan. In his Undelivered Jefferson Day Address of April 11, 1945, Roosevelt states that "More than an end to war, we want an end to the beginnings of all wars."

During this period, the US positioned itself at the forefront of the new internationalism and spearheaded the initiative to create the United Nations in San Francisco. The US was the driving force behind the UN, and it is no accident that its headquarters are in New York. The US set in motion the first international human rights convention, it campaigned for the global monitoring, as well as the judicial and military prosecution, of human rights violations, and it impressed upon the Europeans the idea of a political unification of Europe, initially against French opposition. In the ensuing decades, this period of unprecedented internationalism set in train a wave of innovations in international law that, although blocked during the Cold War, were implemented in part after 1989. Up to that point, it was by no means a foregone conclusion whether the sole remaining superpower would resume its leading role in the march toward a cosmopolitan legal order or regress to the imperial role of a good hegemon above international law.

George Bush, the father of the current president, had different, though admittedly vague, notions of world order from those of his son. The unilateral approach of the current administration and the reputation of its influential neoconservative members and advisors are certainly reminiscent of certain precursors, namely, the rejection of the climate treaty, of the treaty on atomic, biological, and chemical weapons, of the convention on landmines, of the protocols to the agreement on so-called child soldiers, etc. But Kagan asserts a false continuity. The definitive repudiation of internationalism has been the privilege of the current Bush administration: the rejection of the now established International Criminal Court was no peccadillo. However, one should not portray the aggressive marginalization of the United Nations and the flagrant contempt for international law which this administration has on its conscience as the consistent expression of a dominant orientation of American foreign policy. This administration, which has so manifestly failed in its declared goal of defending its national interests, can be voted out of office. What is to prevent it from being replaced next year by an administration that gives the lie to Kagan?[7]

Question: In the United States, the "War on Terrorism" has deteriorated into a "War on Civil Liberties," poisoning the legal infrastructure that makes a vital democratic culture possible. The Orwellian "Patriot Act" is a Pyrrhic victory in which we and our democracy are the victims.

Has the "War on Terrorism" similarly affected the European Union? Or has the experience of terrorism during the 1970s made Europeans immune to the danger of surrendering their civil liberties to the security state?

J. H.: I don't really think so. In West Germany, the reactions in the autumn of 1977 were hysterical enough.[8] Furthermore, we are currently facing a different kind of terrorism. I don't know what would have happened if the Twin Towers had collapsed in Berlin or Frankfurt. Of course, the "security packages" cobbled together in Europe following September 11 have not been so suffocatingly tight or so blatantly unconstitutional as the alarming regulations in America, which, as it happens, have been analyzed unequivocally and skewered by my friend Ronald Dworkin. If we want to draw distinctions in this connection between mentalities and practices on either side of the Atlantic, I would rather look for them at the level of background historical experiences. Perhaps the very understandable shock in the US after September 11 was indeed greater than it would have been in a European country accustomed to war. How could one test this?

Certainly, the patriotic upsurge following the shock of September 11 had an American character. But the key to the curtailment of basic rights to which you allude, to the violation of the Geneva Convention in Guantanamo, to the creation of the Department of Homeland Security, etc., I would locate elsewhere. Consider the militarization of life at home and abroad and the belligerent policies which allow themselves to be infected by the opponent's methods and are restoring the Hobbesian state to the world stage at the very moment when the globalization of markets seemed to have relegated the political element to the wings. The politically astute American populace would never have signed off on all of this by an overwhelming majority if the administration had not taken advantage of the shock of September 11 through pressure tactics, barefaced propaganda, and deliberate fearmongering. For a European observer and a twice-shy child such as me, the systematic intimidation and indoctrination of the population and the restrictions on the spectrum of admissible opinions during October and November 2002 while I was in Chicago were unnerving. This was not "my" America. Since the age of 16, my political thinking has been nourished by the American ideals of the late eighteenth century thanks to the shrewd re-education policy of the Allied occupation administration.

Question: In your keynote address to the World Congress of Philosophy in August 2003 in Istanbul, you said that international security is being threatened in new ways from three sides under the conditions of the postnational constellation: by international terrorism, by criminal states, and by the new civil wars that occur in failed states. What interests me in particular is this: Is terrorism something that democratic states can declare war on?

J. H.: Whether democratic or not, a state can normally wage "war" only against another state, if the word is not to become meaningless. When a government uses military force to quell an insurrection, for example, force fulfils a different function even though the means employed are indeed reminiscent of war. The state is attempting to establish law and order within its own borders under conditions that overtax the normal police organs. Only when this attempt to enforce peace fails and the regime itself degenerates into just one among several contending parties can one speak of "civil war." This verbal analogy to war between states is valid only in one respect: with the collapse of state authority, the same symmetrical relation between opponents which normally obtains between warring states also obtains between the sides in a civil war. Nevertheless, the proper subject of acts of war is missing here, namely, a coercive state authority. Please excuse this conceptual pedantry. But in the case of international terrorism that operates globally and in a

97

dispersed fashion and is for the most part decentralized and only loosely networked, we are dealing with a *new* phenomenon that should not be over-hastily assimilated to what we already know.

Sharon and Putin can feel emboldened by Bush, since he is effacing important distinctions, as though al-Qaeda were no different from the guerrilla campaigns of terrorist independence and resistance movements confined to specific territories (as in Northern Ireland, Palestine, Chechnya, etc.). The al-Qaeda phenomenon is also different from the terrorist gang and tribal warfare conducted by corrupt warlords in the ruins of failed postcolonial states; and it is different from the organized criminality of states that wage war against their own peoples through ethnic cleansing and genocide, or those, like the Taliban, which support global terror. With the war in Iraq, the US government has undertaken not just an illegal but also a futile attempt to substitute an asymmetrical war between states for the asymmetry between a state armed with hi-tech weapons and an elusive terrorist network that has until now operated with knives and explosives. Wars between states are asymmetrical when the victory of an aggressor aiming at the destruction of a regime, rather than a conventional defeat, is determined in advance by the manifest difference in strength between them. Think of the months-long build-up of troops on the borders of Iraq. You don't need to be an expert on terrorism to recognize that this is no way to destroy the infrastructure of a network, to attack the logistics of al-Qaeda and its offshoots, or to deplete the milieus which nourish such a group.

Question: Jurists argue that, according to classical international law, *jus in bello* implies *jus ad bellum* as an inherent constraint. The detailed provisions of the Hague Convention on Wars on Land already sought to set restrictions on wartime violence against the civilian population,

98

against prisoners of war, and against the environment and the infrastructure of the affected society. The rules for the conduct of war are also supposed to make possible a peace treaty acceptable to all parties. However, the obscene disproportion in technological and military strength between the United States and its adversaries in Afghanistan or in Iraq makes it almost impossible to abide by the *jus in bello*. Shouldn't the United States be indicted and prosecuted for the obvious war crimes it has committed in Iraq and which only we here in America are deliberately ignoring?

J. H.: Well, the American Secretary of Defense, Donald Rumsfeld, waxed proudly in precisely this connection that the use of precision weapons supposedly ensured that civilian losses were kept at a relatively low level. But when I read a report in the late edition of the *New York Times* of April 10, 2003 about the Iraqi war dead and Rumsfeld's rules governing acceptable civilian "casualties," then I don't find this alleged precision particularly reassuring: "Air war commanders were required to obtain the approval of Defense Secretary Donald L. Rumsfeld if any planned air strike was thought likely to result in deaths of more than 30 civilians. More than 50 such strikes were proposed and all of them were approved." I don't know what the International Criminal Court in The Hague would have to say about this. But given that this court is not recognized by the US and that no decision of the Security Council can be directed against a member state with veto power, the whole question must be posed differently.

Conservative estimates place the Iraqi dead at around 20,000. This number, which is monstrous when compared with US losses, throws a sharp light on the feeling of moral obscenity that grips us when we see the carefully controlled, even manipulated, images of this asymmetrical war on our television screens. This asymmetry of forces would acquire a completely different significance if it reflected the *police* power of a world organization instead of the overwhelming power and powerlessness of the sides in a *war*.

The Charter of the United Nations already charges it with ensuring peace and international security as well as enforcing individual human rights throughout the world. Let us assume for a moment, counterfactually, that the world organization were up to the task. Then it could fulfill its functions non-selectively only on the condition that it wielded sufficiently powerful sanctions to intimidate rule-violating actors and states. Under these conditions, the asymmetry of power would have assumed a different character.

The extremely onerous and still unlikely transformation of independent and selective punitive wars into police actions authorized by international law requires more than an impartial tribunal adjudicating properly defined crimes. We must also develop the *jus in bello* into a right of intervention that resembles domestic police powers much more closely than the Hague Convention on Wars on Land. The latter remains tailored to acts of *war* rather than to such civil law notions as the obstruction of justice and the execution of sentences. Because innocent lives are always also at stake in humanitarian interventions, the requisite force must be carefully regulated so that the supposed actions of a world police become more than a mere pretext and can thereby gain worldwide acceptance. A good test of this might be the moral feelings of global observers. It is not as though mourning and sympathy could ever disappear; but the spontaneous outrage that many of us felt at the obscene spectacle the sky above Baghdad lit up week after week by missile strikes could become a thing of the past.

Question: John Rawls envisages the possibility that democracies could conduct "just wars" against "outlaw states." But you go further when you argue that even undeniably democratic states may not arrogate to them-

selves the right to wage war against a purportedly despotic, aggressive, or criminal state at their own discretion.
In your Istanbul address, you state that impartial
judgments can never be made by one side alone. For this
cognitive reason alone, the unilateralism of a hegemon,
however well meaning, necessarily lacks legitimacy: "This
defect cannot be made good by the fact that the good
hegemon has a democratic internal constitution." Has the
jus ad bellum, which constituted the core of classical
international law, become obsolete even in the case of the
just war?

J. H.: Rawls's last book, *The Law of Peoples*, has been
justly criticized because he relaxes the strong principles
of justice which a democratic constitution must satisfy
when dealing with authoritarian or semi-authoritarian
states and he places the responsibility for safeguarding
these weakened principles in the hands of individual
democratic states. Rawls cites with approval Michael
Walzer's doctrine of just war in this connection. Both
regard "justice among nations" as desirable and possible,
but they want to entrust the enforcement of international
justice in particular cases to the judgment and discretion
of sovereign states. In this, Rawls seems to share with
Kant the conception of a liberal avant-garde of the community of states; Walzer, by contrast, seems to have in
mind the individual participating nations, quite independently of their internal constitutions. Unlike Rawls,
Walzer's mistrust of supranational procedures and organizations is motivated by communitarian considerations.
Protecting the integrity of the way of life and traditional
ethos of a community organized as a state, as long as it
doesn't resort to genocide and crimes against humanity,
should enjoy precedence over the global enforcement of
abstract principles of justice. The concern underlying
your question can be better addressed in terms of
Walzer's conception than of Rawls's half-hearted defense
of international law.

Since the Kellogg-Briand Pact of 1928, international law has prohibited wars of aggression. It permits the exercise of military force only in cases of self-defense. The *jus ad bellum*, as understood by classical international law, was thereby abolished. Because the institutions of the League of Nations founded after World War I proved to be too weak, after World War II the United Nations was vested with the authority to conduct peacekeeping operations and to impose sanctions, although at the cost of veto rights for the major powers of the time. The UN Charter stipulates that international law takes precedence over the legal systems of the various nations. The coupling of the Charter with the Declaration of Human Rights, and the wide-ranging authority enjoyed by the Security Council under Chapter VII, set off a wave of legal innovations which, even though they remained an unused "fleet in being" until 1989, have been correctly interpreted as a "constitutionalizing of international law." The world organization, which in the meantime comprises 193 member states, has a genuine constitution that lays down the procedures in accordance with which international breaches of the rules can be ascertained and punished. Since then, we no longer have just and unjust wars, only legal or illegal ones, depending on whether they are justified or unjustified under international law.

One must bear this enormous advance in the evolution of law in mind in order to grasp the radical breach wrought by the Bush administration – as much with its security doctrine, which willfully ignores the relevant legal preconditions for the exercise of military force, as with its ultimatum to the Security Council either to give its blessing to the United States' aggressive Iraq policy or sink into irrelevance. In the rhetoric of legitimation, this was not a case of a "realist" dismissal of "idealist" notions. Insofar as the Bush administration wanted to eliminate an unjust system and democratize the Middle East, its normative aims were not contrary to the program of the United Nations. In dispute was not the question of whether justice

102

between nations is possible in principle, but only how to accomplish it. The Bush administration has laid the 220-year-old Kantian project of *juridifying* international relations *ad acta* with empty moralistic phrases.

The behavior of the American government admits only one conclusion, namely, that from their point of view international law is finished as a medium for resolving conflicts between states and for promoting democracy and human rights. The superpower now makes these goals the official centerpiece of a policy that no longer appeals to law but to its own ethical values and moral convictions. It substitutes its own normative rationales for prescribed judicial procedures. But the one cannot replace the other. The renunciation of legal argument always signals the abandonment of previously recognized general norms. From the restricted viewpoint of its own political culture and its own understanding of itself and the world, even the most considerate and well-intentioned hegemon cannot be certain that it understands and is taking account of the interests and situation of the other affected parties. This holds for the citizens of a democratic superpower no less than for its political leadership. Without inclusive legal procedures open to all of the parties involved that enjoin them to reciprocal perspective-taking, the dominant party is under no compulsion to give up the central vantage point of a large empire or to engage in the degree of decentering of interpretive perspectives demanded by the conceptual constraints of granting equal consideration to the interests of all.

Even an ultra-modern power like the US relapses into the pseudo-universalism of the ancient empires when it substitutes morality and ethics for positive law in issues of international justice. From Bush's perspective, "our" values are universally valid values that all other nations should accept in their own best interests. This pseudo-universalism is a kind of universalized ethnocentrism. Moreover, a theory of just war derived from theological and natural law traditions has nothing to set against this,

103

even when it appears in its current communitarian garb. I am not saying that the official rationales of the American government for the Iraq War, or even the officially expressed religious convictions of the American president concerning "good" and "evil," satisfy the Walzerian criteria for a "just war." Walzer in his role as political commentator has left nobody in the dark on that score.[9] However, Walzer-the-philosopher derives his criteria, however reasonable they may be, exclusively from moral principles and ethical considerations outside the context of a theory of law that ties judgments on war and peace to inclusive and impartial procedures for generating and applying binding norms.

In the present context, what interests me is just one implication of such an approach, namely, that the criteria for judging just wars are not translated into the medium of law. Only in this way can inevitably controversial substantive notions of "justice" be translated into the verifiable criteria of the legality of wars. Walzer's criteria for just wars are essentially ethical and political in nature, even when they constitute part of international customary law. Their application in particular cases is not subject to verification by international courts of law and remains a matter for the sagacity and sense of justice of individual states.

But why should the impartial adjudication of conflicts in the medium of law be valid only within states? What is to prevent the application of this medium to international conflicts in formal judicial proceedings? The point is really trivial: who is to determine at the supranational level whether "our" values actually merit universal acceptance or whether we are in fact applying universally recognized principles impartially – whether our perception of a conflict situation is really non-selective, for example, rather than only taking into consideration what is relevant for us? This is the whole point of inclusive legal procedures that make supranational decision-making conditional upon reciprocal perspectives and consideration of interests.

Question: With all due respect to your Kantian project, isn't it leading you to advocate a form of "military humanism?"

J. H.: I don't know the precise context of that expression, but I imagine that it is an allusion to the danger of a moralization of the relation between adversaries. At the international level in particular, a demonizing of adversaries – think of the "axis of evil" – does not exactly promote conflict resolution. Fundamentalism is currently gaining ground on all sides, lending conflicts in Iraq, Israel, and elsewhere a fatal character. As it happens, Carl Schmitt also presented this argument in defense of a "non-discriminatory concept of war" throughout his career. Insofar as classical international law viewed war as a legitimate means of resolving interstate conflicts that needed no further justification, he argued, it fulfilled an important precondition for civilizing wars. By criminalizing wars of aggression, the Versailles Treaty first made war itself a crime and then set in train a dynamic of "derestriction" [*Entgrenzung*] by transforming adversaries, who are morally condemned, into despicable enemies to be annihilated. When the moralization of war prevents the parties from respecting each other as honorable adversaries – i.e. as *justus hostis* – limited wars degenerate into total wars.

This argument is not wrong, even though total war dates more from the era of nationalistic mass-mobilizations and the development of weapons of mass destruction. However, it merely reinforces my thesis that one cannot achieve "justice between nations" through moralization but only through the juridification of international relations. The discriminatory judgment only fosters strife when one party presumes to pass judgment *according to its own standards* upon the alleged crimes of the other party. We must not confuse this kind of subjective judgment with the judicial condemnation of a proven criminal regime and its henchmen before the forum of a community of nations equipped with a constitution. For the latter extends the protection of the law also to an accused party who enjoys the presumption of innocence until proven guilty.

Admittedly, this distinction between the moralization and the legalization of international relations would not have satisfied Carl Schmitt. For him and his fascist fellow-travelers, the existential struggle to the death possessed a weird vitalistic aura. Schmitt thought that the substance of the political, the self-assertion of the identity of a people or a movement, cannot be tamed by norms and that any attempt to domesticate it through law must lead to moral degeneracy. Even if legal pacifism were to succeed, it would rob us of the essential means for renewing an authentic existence. However, we don't need to concern ourselves further here with this abstruse conception of the political.

We do need to concern ourselves with the purportedly "realistic" premise defended by Hobbesians both of the left and the right, namely, that law, even in the modern guise of constitutional democracy, is merely a reflex and mask for economic or political power. On this assumption, legal pacifism, which seeks to extend law to the international state of nature, is a sheer illusion. In fact, the Kantian project of constitutionalizing international law is nourished by an idealism free from illusions. The form of modern law as such has an unambiguous moral core that proves itself in the long run as a "gentle civilizer" (Koskenniemi) whenever law is employed as the medium in which a constitution is formed.

The egalitarian universalism immanent in law and its procedures has left discernible empirical traces on the political and social reality of the West. For the idea of equal treatment invested in both the law of peoples and the law of states can fulfill ideological functions only by also serving as the standard for the critique of ideology. For this reason, today opposition and liberation movements across the world adopt the vocabulary of human rights. Moreover, as soon as the rhetoric of human rights is misused for the purposes of oppression and exclusion, it can be invoked against this very misuse.

Question: Precisely as an unconditional defender of the Kantian project, you must be deeply disappointed by the Machiavellian machinations that so often dominate the activity of the United Nations. You yourself have drawn attention to the "shameful selectivity" exhibited by the Security Council in even registering and dealing with cases where it ought to take action. You speak of the shameful "primacy still enjoyed by national interests over the global obligations of the international community."[10] What alterations and reforms should the institutions of the United Nations undergo so that a shield for the uni-lateral pursuit of pro-Western interests and goals can develop into an effective tool for securing peace?

J. H.: That's a big topic. Institutional reforms are not suf-ficient. Reconfiguring the Security Council so that it ade-quately reflects the altered power relations, a proposal currently under discussion, and the restriction of the veto right of the major powers are certainly necessary, but they don't go far enough. Let me single out a couple of aspects of this unwieldy complex.

The world organization is rightly committed to full inclusiveness. It remains open to all nations that commit themselves to the *wording* of the UN Charter and to the declarations that are binding in international law, ir-respective of the degree to which their own domestic practices actually accord with these principles. Hence, measured by their own normative principles, there exists a gradation in legitimacy between liberal, semi-authoritarian, and even despotic member states, in spite of the formal equality enjoyed by all members. This becomes apparent when, for example, a country like Libya assumes the chairmanship of the Human Rights Commission. John Rawls deserves credit for having pointed out this fundamental problem of graduated legitimation. The superiority in terms of legitimacy enjoyed by democratic countries, on which Kant already rested his hopes, hardly lends itself to formalization. Nevertheless, customs and practices could develop that take account of it. This also underlines the need to reform the veto rights of the permanent members of the Security Council.

The most pressing problem, of course, is the restricted scope for action of a world organization that does not enjoy a monopoly on the use of force and must depend on the ad hoc support of powerful member states, especially in cases of intervention and nation building. However, the problem does not lie in the lack of a monopoly on force. The differentiation between the constitution and executive authority can also be observed elsewhere, in the European Union, for example, where EU law trumps national law, even though the nation-states continue to control the means of legitimate force held in reserve. Aside from its financial underfunding, the United Nations suffers above all from its dependency on governments that not only pursue their respective national interests but also depend on the support of their national publics. Until the self-perception of member states that still view themselves as sovereign actors undergoes a transformation at the social-cognitive level, we must think about how we can achieve a relative uncoupling of levels of decision-making. For example, the member states could make contingents of troops available expressly for UN purposes without constraining their national rights of control over their own military forces.

However, we can only realistically pursue the ambitious goal of a world domestic politics without a world government if the UN confines itself to its two most important functions, maintaining peace and enforcing human rights globally, and leaves political coordination in the areas of the economy, the environment, transportation, health, etc., to mid-level institutions and negotiation systems. But at present this level of global players who could take political initiatives and negotiate compromises with each other is represented by just a handful of institutions, such as the World Trade Organization. A reform of the United Nations, however successful, would remain ineffectual unless the nation-states in the various world regions come together to form continental regimes on the model of the European Union. For the moment, only modest steps have been taken in this direction. Herein, and not in the reform of the UN, lies the genuinely utopian moment of a "cosmopolitan condition."

The legitimation needs of an empowered UN might even be met in a halfway democratic manner by a division of labor within such a multilevel global system. Until now, a global political public sphere has formed only intermittently in response to major historical events like September 11. However, it could one day assume a more concrete institutional form and greater continuity thanks to the electronic media and the striking successes of global non-governmental organizations, such as Amnesty International and Human Rights Watch. Under such circumstances, the idea of establishing a "parliament of world citizens" (David Held) alongside the "second chamber" of the General Assembly – or, barring that, at least an expansion of the existing chamber of states to include a representation of citizens – would no longer be absurd. This would set a symbolic and institutional seal on an evolution in international law that has been in progress for a long time. For not only states but also citizens themselves have become subjects of international law; as world citizens, they can even assert legal claims against their own governments if need be.

To be sure, an idea as abstract as that of a parliament of world citizens is dizzying. However, one must bear in mind that, given the limited functions of the United Nations, the delegates to this parliament would represent populations that do not need to be bound together by thick traditions like the citizens of a political community. A negative consensus would suffice in place of civic

109

solidarity, namely, shared outrage at the aggressive war-mongering and human rights violations of criminal gangs and regimes or shared horror over acts of ethnic cleansing and genocide.

Admittedly, the resistances and setbacks which have to be overcome along the way to full constitutionalization are so great that the project can only succeed if the US once again positions itself at the forefront as the driving force of the movement, as it did in 1945. This is not as improbable as it may now appear. For one thing, it is a lucky accident of world history that the sole superpower is the oldest democracy on earth and hence has, contrary to what Kagan would have us believe, "elective affinities" with the Kantian idea of a legal domestication of international relations. For another, it is in the interest of the United States itself to invest the UN with decision-making power before another, less democratic, major power rises to superpower status. Empires come and go. After all, the European Union has just agreed on principles of security and a defense policy that contrast a notion of "preventive engagements" with the "pre-emptive strikes" outlawed by international law. It could thereby exercise an influence on the political public opinion of our American ally.

Question: The contempt of the American government for international law and international treaties, the brutal exercise of military force, and a politics of deception and blackmail have provoked an anti-Americanism that, insofar as it is directed at the current administration, is not unfounded. How should Europe respond to this spreading animus to ensure that the worldwide anti-Americanism does not rebound on the West as a whole in a wave of hatred?

J. H.: Anti-Americanism is a danger in Europe itself. In Germany, it has always allied itself with the most reactionary movements. Hence, it is important for us, as during the Vietnam War, to be able to make common cause with an American domestic opposition against the policies of the American government. If we can point to a protest movement within the United States itself, the counter-productive charge of anti-Americanism leveled against us also loses its force. The anti-modernist sentiment directed against the West as a whole is another matter. This calls for self-criticism, let us say, a self-critical defense of the achievements of Western modernity that signals both openness and a willingness to learn and above all overcomes the idiotic equation of democratic order and liberal society with unbridled capitalism. On the one hand, we must take a clear stand against fundamentalism, including Christian and Jewish fundamentalism, and, on the other, we must acknowledge that fundamentalism is the child of disruptive processes of modernization in which the aberrations of our colonial history and the failures of decolonization played a decisive role. We can at any rate make clear against such fundamentalist fixations that justified criticism of the West derives its standards from the West's own 200-year-old discourse of self-criticism.

Question: Two political agendas have recently fallen victim to war and terrorism: the so-called "road map," which was supposed to lead to peace between the Israelis and the Palestinians, and the imperialist scenario of Cheney, Rumsfeld, Rice, and Bush. The script for the conflict in Israel was supposed to be written in tandem with the script for reconstructing the entire Middle East. But the policies of the United States have succeeded in fusing anti-Americanism with anti-Semitism. Today anti-Americanism is feeding old forms of murderous anti-Semitism. How can we defuse this explosive mixture?

J. H.: This is a problem, particularly in Germany where at present the floodgates of a narcissistic preoccupation with its own war victims are opening and a necessary censorship exercised for decades by official opinion against

111

popular prejudices is beginning to break down. But we will only be able to come to grips with the mixture which you quite correctly describe if we succeed in keeping the legitimate task of criticizing Bush's fatal vision of global order free in a convincing manner from every admixture of anti-Americanism. Once the *other* America again assumes discernible contours, it will also pull the ground out from under the anti-Americanism that merely serves as a disguise for anti-Semitism.

IV
The Kantian Project and the Divided West

8
Does the Constitutionalization of International Law Still Have a Chance?[1]

Introduction

As the European system of states was taking shape, philosophy, in the persons of Francisco Suarez, Hugo Grotius, and Samuel Pufendorf, still played the role of pacemaker in the creation of modern international law. Moreover, when legally constrained international relations later stabilized at the level of violence of so-called cabinet wars [*Kabinettskriege*], philosophy assumed this role a second time. With his conception of a "cosmopolitan condition" or "*weltbürgerlichen Zustand,*" Kant took a decisive step beyond international law centered exclusively on states. Since then, international law has not only developed into a specialized brand of legal theory. Following two world wars, the constitutionalization of international law has evolved along the lines prefigured by Kant toward cosmopolitan law and has assumed institutional form in international constitutions, organizations, and procedures.[2]

Since the end of the bipolar world order and the emergence of the US as the pre-eminent world power, an alternative to the evolution of a cosmopolitan constitution has emerged. A world dominated by nation-states is indeed in transition toward the postnational constellation of a global society. States are losing their autonomy in part as they become increasingly enmeshed in the horizontal

115

networks of a global society.³ But in this situation the Kantian project of a cosmopolitan order not only has to confront the traditional objection of "realists" who affirm the quasi-ontological primacy of brute power over law. Other opponents are currently emerging who advocate the liberal ethos of a superpower as an *alternative* to law.

On the realist conception, the normative taming of political power through law is possible only within the confines of a sovereign state whose existence is founded on its capacity to assert itself with force. On this premise, international law must forever lack the cutting edge of a law armed with sanctions. Today, a more far-reaching conflict is superseding the dispute between Kantian ideal- ists and realists of the Carl Schmitt school over the limits to the juridification of international relations.⁴ The project of a new liberal world order under the banner of a *pax Americana* advocated by the neoconservative masterminds of the current US administration raises the question of whether the *juridification* of international relations should be superseded by a *moralization* of international politics grounded in the ethos of a superpower.

Idealists and realists clashed over whether justice is even possible in relations between nations;⁵ the new dispute, by contrast, is over whether law remains an appropriate medium for realizing the declared goals of achieving peace and international security and promoting democracy and human rights throughout the world. Now the controversy concerns the path by which we can achieve these goals, whether via the legally established procedures of an inclusive, but often weak and selective, world orga- nization, or via the unilaterally imposed decisions of a well-meaning hegemon. At first glance, events seemed to have settled the issue when Saddam's statue was toppled from its pedestal in Baghdad. By then the US government had ignored international law twice, first with its procla- mation of a National Security Strategy in September 2002 and then with the invasion of Iraq in March 2003. In addition, it had sidelined the United Nations in order to accord priority to its own, ethically rather than legally, justified national interests, even over the objections of its allies. The marginalization of the world organization by a superpower bent on going to war represented a dramatic challenge to existing law.

Hence, the question arises of whether there is anything amiss, normatively speaking, in this imperial approach, assuming, at least for the sake of argument, that the American action could have realized more effectively the same goals which the United Nations had hitherto pursued half-heartedly and with scant success. Or, even granting this counterfactual assumption, should we not rather hold steadfastly to the alternative project of a constitutionalization of international law and do our utmost to bring a future US government to recall the world-historical mission embraced by Presidents Wilson and Roosevelt, in each case following a calamitous world war? For the Kantian project can only continue if the US returns to the internationalism it embraced after 1918 and 1945 and once again assumes the role of pacemaker in the evolution of international law toward a "cosmopolitan condition."

A situation marked by terrorism and war and by disparities in global economic development that are merely amplified by the unfortunate consequences of the Iraq War compels us to reflect anew on this issue. Granted, nowadays philosophy can at most play the ancillary role of elucidating the concepts employed in the specialized treatments of international lawyers and political scientists. Whereas the role of political science is to describe the state of international relations and that of jurisprudence is to give an account of the concept, validity, and content of international law, philosophy can try to clarify certain basic conceptual features of the development of law in the light of both existing constellations and valid norms. Only at this level can it contribute to the discussion of whether the Kantian project still has a future.

117

Before returning to this question at the end of the chapter, I would like in the first part to detach the idea of the cosmopolitan condition from its conceptual linkage with the concrete notion of a world republic. In the second, historically oriented part, I will examine the trends which have promoted or hindered the constitutionalization of international law, properly understood.

Politically Constituted World Society vs. World Republic

Classical international law and "sovereign equality"

Kant deplores the idea of wars of aggression[6] and questions the right of sovereign states to go to war, i.e. the *jus ad bellum*. This "right," which is "strictly speaking, unintelligible,"[7] constitutes the structural core of classical international law. This set of rules derived from customary law and treaties reflects the contours of the European state system which took shape following the Peace of Westphalia and remained in place roughly until 1914. With the exception of the Vatican, only states – and until the middle of the nineteenth century only European states – were admitted. Thus tailored exclusively to the participation of "nations," classical international law was constitutive for "inter-national" relations in the literal sense. It represents nation-states as participants in a strategic game:

- states enjoy sufficient *de facto* independence to make autonomous choices and act on their own preferences;
- guided by the imperatives of self-assertion and self-defense, they pursue exclusively their own preferences (understood as "national interests") and the security of their citizens;
- any state can form coalitions with any other state and they all compete to increase their political power through their ability to exert military threats.

International law lays down the rules of the game[8] and determines:

(a)   the qualifications that potential participants must satisfy: a sovereign state must be able to exercise effective control over its social and territorial boundaries and maintain law and order;

(b)   the admission requirements: state sovereignty rests on international recognition; and

(c)   the actual status: a sovereign state can conclude treaties with other states. When conflicts arise, it has the right to declare war on other states without offering supporting reasons (*jus ad bellum*), but it may not intervene in the internal affairs of other states (the prohibition on intervention).

These principles entail a series of consequences:

- there is no supranational authority to sanction and punish violations of international law;
- a sovereign state can violate standards of prudence and efficiency, but it cannot violate moral norms: its behavior is treated as morally indifferent;
- the immunity enjoyed by states extends to their representatives, officials, and functionaries;
- sovereign states reserve the right to prosecute and try crimes committed in war (in accordance with the *jus in bello*);
- third parties may remain neutral vis-à-vis warring parties.

Thus, the normative content of classical international law extends only to according equal status to sovereign states, a status that rests on the reciprocal recognition of subjects of international law, without regard to differences in size of population, territory, and actual political or economic power. The price for this "sovereign equality" is the acceptance of war as the mechanism for regulating conflicts and thus the freedom to resort to military force. This precludes the possibility of higher impartial judicial and prosecutorial authorities. These two features account for the "soft" character of international law, whose effectiveness remains dependent in the final analysis on the sovereign will of contracting parties. The efficacy of international treaties is subject in principle to the qualification that the sovereign parties reserve the right to substitute politics for law whenever they see fit.

The political constellation underlying classical international law is different from that underlying state law. The power of the state which secures the rights of citizens is itself bound by law. At the national level, the political authority of the state, which is first constituted in the forms of law, and law, which is contingent on the sanctioning power of the state, are *mutually interdependent*. This interdependence of "political power" and "law" is absent at the international level, where an asymmetrical relation between power and law persists because international legal regulations reflect the underlying power constellations between states without normatively transforming them. Law expresses and, in certain respects, shapes relations between sovereign powers, but it does not effectively constrain them.

Hence, classical international law can exercise an inherent stabilizing effect only to the extent that the formally equal status of the subjects of international law is "backed" by a *de facto* balance of powers, always assuming that warring parties accept a tacit agreement to respect certain limits on the use of violence in war as morally sacrosanct. Kant contests both of these assumptions on empirical grounds. With the contemporary example of the division of Poland in mind, he describes the role of the balance of power in promoting peace as a "mere fantasy."[9] And it is not only the horrors of "wars of punishment and extermination" that are a moral scandal for Kant. Even cabinet wars conducted with standing armies are incompatible "with the right of humanity in our own person," because a state that hires its citizens "to kill or be killed" degrades them into "mere machines."[10]

Peace as an implication of law-governed freedom

The abolition of war is a command of reason. Practical reason first brings the moral veto to bear against systematic killing: *"there is to be no war,* neither war between you and me in the state of nature nor war between us as states, which, although they are internally in a lawful condition, are still externally (in relation to one another) in a lawless condition."[11] For Kant, however, law is not merely a suitable *means* for establishing peace between states; rather, he conceives of peace between nations from the beginning in terms of legal peace.[12] This is an important difference between Kant and Hobbes.

Like Hobbes, Kant insists on the *conceptual* connection between law and securing peace. However, in contrast with Hobbes, he does not trace the legal pacification of society back to the paradigmatic pledge of obedience by the subjects of law in return for the state's guarantee of protection. From Kant's republican perspective, there is instead a conceptual connection between the role of law in promoting peace and the role of a legal condition that citizens can accept as legitimate in promoting freedom. The cosmopolitan extension of a condition of civil liberties first secured within the constitutional state is not only pursued because it gives rise to perpetual peace, but also for its own sake, as a command of practical reason. Hence, "establishing universal and lasting peace constitutes not merely a part . . . but rather the final end of the doctrine of right." The idea of a *"peaceful,* even if not yet friendly, thoroughgoing community of all nations" is a principle of right, not merely a command of morality.[13] The cosmopolitan condition is just the condition of peace made permanent. The idea of the cosmopolitan constitution which guarantees "a union of all peoples under public laws" has the meaning of a "genuine," definitive, and not merely provisional condition of peace.

This conceptual connection between the telos of peace and the principle of law also explains the "cosmopolitan intent" of the philosophy of history, and hence the heuristic standpoint from which Kant deciphers the course of history: "The problem of establishing a perfect civil constitution depends on the problem of law-governed external relations among nations and cannot be solved unless the latter is."[14]

The reference to a "civil constitution" here is crucial: international law, which regulates interactions among states, must be superseded by the constitution of a community of states. Only then will states and their citizens enter into a "law-governed relation" to one another.

By a "law-governed relation" Kant means one in which the freedom of each coexists with the freedom of everyone else in accordance with a universal law.[15] It is important to note that Kant shares Rousseau's material concept of law.[16] Laws satisfy the conditions of a pragmatic, and not merely a semantic, universality when they are the result of an inclusive procedure of will-formation marked by discussion and publicity.[17] The danger of despotism lurking in all laws that are merely imposed from above can only be averted by a republican procedure, namely, a fair process of opinion- and will-formation among all those potentially affected. The laws of the international community, too, will only take *equal* account of the interests of all states – regardless of their size and population, their wealth and their political and economic power – when they give expression to a will that is "united" because it has arisen through an analogously inclusive procedure.[18]

Kant uses the analogy of a "civil constitution" [*staatsbürgerliche Verfassung*] to lend concrete content to the general idea of a "cosmopolitan constitution" [*weltbürgerliche Verfassung*] in the sense of a "universal state of nations." In his bold outline of a cosmopolitan order, he takes his inspiration from the revolutionary constitution-founding acts of his time. The republics which emerged from the American and French Revolutions were the first and, at that time, the only examples of a form of law-giving that satisfied republican standards of legitimacy, "since all decide about all, hence each about himself; for it is only to oneself that one can never do wrong."[19] From this perspective, a *constitution* for the international community was conceivable only in the form of a republic of republics, that is, as a "republicanism of all states"[20] or as a "world republic."[21] In this way, the constitution of the nation-state realized through revolution becomes the model for the transition from classical international law to cosmopolitan law – and misleads Kant into an overhasty concretization of the general idea of a "cosmopolitan condition" or a constitution for the international community. In fact, there is no need to interpret the goal of a constitutionalization of international law in terms of a world republic.

From the law of states to the rights of world citizens

Before examining the problematic consequences of this rash move, I would like to clarify the cosmopolitan meaning of the construct of a world republic. This construction renders war as a legitimate means of resolving conflicts, indeed war *as such*, impossible, because there cannot be "external" conflicts within a globally inclusive commonwealth. What had hitherto been military conflicts would assume the character of police actions and operations of criminal justice. Kant recognized, however, that the idea of a world republic could degenerate into something different from a supranational legal order to which governments submit themselves, by analogy with the republican legal order among individual human beings.[22] After all, a "universal monarchy" could also bring about a legal pacification of world society by repressive means, that is, through a despotic monopoly of power. The idea of a cosmopolitan condition is more demanding because it projects the institutionalization of civil rights from the national level onto the international level.

The core innovation of this idea consists in the transformation of international law as a law of *states* into cosmopolitan law as a law of *individuals*. The latter are no longer legal subjects merely as citizens of their respective states, but also as members of a "cosmopolitan commonwealth under a single head."[23] The civil rights of individual persons are now supposed to penetrate international relations too. The price paid by sovereign states uniting to form a "large state body" for promoting their citizens to world citizens is that they must submit to a higher authority. In acquiring the status of members of a republic of republics, they renounce the option of substituting politics for law in their dealings with other member states. The imposition of the format of a state on international relations would mean that law completely permeates and transforms political power, even in external relations among states. The difference between external and internal sovereignty would thereby disappear, not only on account of the global scale of the inclusive state of nations, but also for normative reasons: the binding force of the republican constitution would disperse the "substance" of the state's "wild," legally untamed power of self-assertion toward other states. "Political" power, in the sense of an executive power conserved "behind" the law, would lose its last domain of untrammeled exercise with the eclipse of the international stage.

Over the course of his career, Kant never actually renounced the *idea* of a complete constitutionalization of international law in the form of a world republic. There has been much speculation over why, in his essay "Toward Perpetual Peace," he nevertheless introduced the weaker conception of a league or confederation of nations [*Völkerbund*] and thereafter pinned his hopes on a voluntary association of states which are morally committed to peace while remaining legally sovereign. The notorious passage in which he justifies this step reads as follows:

> In accordance with reason there is only one way that states . . . can leave the lawless condition . . . ; it is that . . . they give up their savage (lawless) freedom, accommodate themselves to public coercive laws, and so form a . . . state of nations that would finally encompass all the nations on earth. But since, in accordance with their idea of the right of nations, they do not at all want this, so . . . in place of the positive idea of a world republic only the negative surrogate of a league that averts war . . . can stem the tide of hostile inclinations.[24]

Associated with the project of a league of nations is the idea of an ever-expanding federation of republics engaging in commerce which renounce wars of aggression and accept a moral obligation to submit conflicts among themselves to an international court of arbitration, while reserving the right to withdraw at any time. With this project of a permanent congress of states – which would materialize two decades later in the quite different form of the counter-revolutionary "Holy Alliance" – Kant by no means repudiates the idea of a cosmopolitan condition as such.[25] As always, he relies on the course of history, which, beginning with the taming of military violence by international law, and proceeding through the prohibition of wars of aggression, would finally approach the goal of constructing a cosmopolitan constitution. However, Kant judged that the nations were not yet sufficiently mature and needed to undergo further learning processes. Even today there is ample empirical evidence for the fact that nation-states cling to their sovereignty, that they "do not at all want" to give up the freedom of action granted them by classical international law. Yet, for Kant, this was not a sufficient reason to abandon the *idea* itself. Ideas in the strict sense always transcend the historical situations they illuminate through practical imperatives.

Kant does not generally respond to historical obstacles by introducing a "surrogate" for such an idea. Instead, he appeals to the philosophy of history to situate the idea within a rich context of *accommodating trends*.[26] As is well known, he pins his hopes primarily on three long-term factors:

- the peaceful character of republics, which will form the avant-garde of the league of nations;
- the pacifying effect of free trade, which makes state actors dependent on the growing interdependences of the world market and compels them to cooperate with one another; and
- the critical function of an emergent global public sphere that mobilizes the conscience and political participation of citizens all over the world, because "violations of law in one place of the earth are felt in all."[27]

Although these trends can be reversed at any time, in the long run obstacles will be overcome. Hence, they do not compel Kant to modify the idea itself. However, if the latter finds its proper expression in a federal world republic, why then does he entertain the project of a league of nations at all?

Why the "surrogate" of the league of nations?

In proposing a *league* of nations as a surrogate for the *state* of nations, Kant seems to be reacting to difficulties of a conceptual rather than an empirical order. Moreover, these conceptual problems prove to be the most instructive when we consider in hindsight the actual, though always precarious, progress of the constitutionalization of international law since the end of World War I. They reveal that, although Kant had good reasons for his idea of a transformation of state-centered international law

126

toward cosmopolitan law, he did not develop it in sufficiently abstract terms. That idea was so closely bound up
with the image of a world republic or a state of nations
that it was inevitably discredited when confronted with
the asymmetrical distribution of power and the overwhelming complexity of a world society marked by striking socioeconomic disparities and cultural divisions.

Kant justifies the project of the league of nations
[*Völkerbund*] by arguing that the concept of the state of
nations [*Völkerstaat*] proves to be inconsistent on closer
examination:

> That would be a contradiction inasmuch as every state
> involves the relation of a *superior* (legislating) to an *inferior*
> (obeying, namely the people); but a number of nations
> in one state would constitute only one nation, and this
> contradicts the presupposition (since here we have to
> consider the right of *nations* in relation to one another
> insofar as they comprise different states and are not to be
> fused into a single state).[28]

In this context, Kant appears to treat "states" not only as
associations of free and equal citizens in conformity with
the individualism of modern constitutional law, but also
in ethical-political terms, that is, as national communities.
These collectivities consist of "peoples" or "nations" (itali-
cized in the original) that are differentiated from one
another by language, religion, and mode of life. The loss
of the sovereignty of their state would mean for each of
them the loss of the kind of independence already acquired
by nations that form a political community of their own.
The autonomy of their respective collective forms of life
would thereby be jeopardized. On this reading, the "contradiction" resides in the fact that the price the citizens
of a world republic would have to pay for the legal guarantee of peace and civil liberties would be the loss of
the substantive ethical freedom they enjoy as members
of a national community organized as an independent
nation-state.

In fact, this supposed contradiction, over which generations of Kant interpreters have racked their brains,[29]
dissolves once we examine the premise underlying the
argument. Kant takes the French republic as his model
and is forced into an unnecessary conceptual bind by the
dogma of the indivisibility of state sovereignty.[30] Although
"all authority proceeds from the people," this authority is
already split at source in the constitutional state with its
division of powers. The people cannot rule directly but
(as stated in the German Basic Law, Article 20, Paragraph
2) it exercises governmental authority [*Staatsgewalt*]
"through elections and other votes and through specific
legislative, executive, and judicial bodies." Given this
proceduralist conception of popular sovereignty, in a federalist multilevel system nothing prevents the fictive unity
of the presumptive popular sovereign from being conceived as compatible with the corresponding chains of
legitimation that unfold in parallel within each of the
various member states.[31] Had Kant read this conception
of "divided" sovereignty from the US model, he would
have realized that the "peoples" of independent states who
restrict their sovereignty for the sake of a federal government need not sacrifice their distinct cultural identities.

Even this conception does not completely dispel the
concern that peoples "divided" by religion and language
would be "fused" in a world republic. Kant's concern that
in a highly complex world society general laws could be
enforced only at the cost of a "soulless despotism" prefig-
ures something akin to Foucault's fear of "normalization."
Kant fears that a world republic, notwithstanding its
federal structure, would inevitably lead to social and cultural uniformity. Behind this fear lurks the objection that
a global state of nations would develop an inherent, irre-
sistible tendency to degenerate into a "universal monarchy" for sheer functional reasons. Kant seems to be
concerned that the alternative to the existing system of
belligerent sovereign states would be the global domination of a single world power. It is this alternative that

128

ultimately leads him to resort to the surrogate conception of a "league of nations."

The misleading analogy of the state of nature

This raises the question of whether the alternative itself is correctly posed. Kant arrives at the alternative of a world republic or world government by an analogy that leads him to an over-hasty, concretistic interpretation of the idea of a "cosmopolitan condition" in terms of a global state or world republic. The anarchic character of international relations in which sovereign states find themselves suggests a comparison with the "state of nature," familiar from social contract theory, in which pre-social individuals are supposed to have found themselves.[32] The social contract teaches them that the only way out of their wretched condition of unremitting insecurity is to organize themselves as citizens of a state. Likewise, it seems that states must now seek an analogous way out of a similarly untenable state of nature.[33] Just as individual persons previously renounced their natural freedom to unite into a commonwealth under coercive laws organized as a state, so too individual states must in turn renounce their sovereignty and form a "cosmopolitan commonwealth under a single head." Just as the state was the solution to the first problem, so too a state of states – a state of nations or a world republic – is supposed to provide a solution to this problem.

However, this analogy is misleading, even on the premises of Kant's own social contract theory.[34] In contrast to individuals in the state of nature, citizens of competing states already enjoy a status that guarantees them rights and liberties (however restricted). The disanalogy is rooted in the fact that citizens of any state have already undergone a long process of political formation and socialization. They possess the political good of legally secured freedoms which they would jeopardize if they were to accept restrictions on the sovereign power of the state which guarantees this legal condition. The pre-social inhabitants of the state of nature had nothing to lose but the fear and terror generated by the clash of their natural, and hence insecure, freedoms. Therefore, the curriculum that states and their citizens must undergo in the transition from classical international law to a cosmopolitan condition is *complementary*, rather than *analogous*, to the curriculum in which citizens of constitutional states have already graduated in the course of the juridification of an initially unconstrained state power.

The idea of the social contract represents an attempt to reconstruct conceptually the emergence of the state as the organizational form of legitimate political authority. State-organized authority consists in the exercise of political power through the administration of binding law. From a conceptual point of view, governmental authority has two components, a quasi-natural, hence initially pre-political, power of command, on the one hand, and the rule structure and binding force of an originally metasocially grounded law, on the other.[35] As the source of collectively binding decisions, *political* power results from the fusion of these two components. Political power is constituted in the form of law. In stabilizing behavioral expectations (and thereby fulfilling its specific function), law puts its rule structure at the service of power. To this extent, law serves as the means by which power is organized. At the same time, it provides a resource of justice from which power can simultaneously legitimate itself. While political power thereby derives its sustenance from law, law in turn owes its compulsory character to the sanctioning power of the state. There can be no rule of law without recourse to the means of force held in reserve as the guarantee of political domination.

Modern natural law emerged in the seventeenth century in the form of social contract theory. In the wake of the wars of religion, it was supposed to provide an interpretation of a system of states that reconfigured itself around religiously neutral grounds of legitimation. Rational natural law provides a critical analysis of the conceptual constellation of law and power whose aim is to make explicit the egalitarian content which had until then remained implicit in the legal medium of a more or less authoritarian form of political power. Rousseau and Kant decode this latent rational content of a law that had thus far only been instrumentalized for political purposes by means of their innovative concept of autonomy. They trace the legitimating function of the *form* of fully positivized law back to the generality of legal norms, understood in more than merely semantic terms, and ultimately to the legitimacy-generating procedure of democratic legislation.[36] This conception of rational, i.e. democratically generated, law was to reveal the normative dynamic intrinsic to the very form of modern law which enables this medium to *rationalize* the substance of an arbitrary political domination and not merely to lend it a *rational appearance*. The point of the reconstructive program of social contract theory was to demonstrate that the conceptual germ of the constitutionalization of the "irrational," unregulated decisionistic power of the state is, in virtue of its formal legal character, already implicit in political power itself.

According to this view, the interpenetration of positive law and political power aims not at the legal type of modern government as such but at a democratically constituted rule of law. The *terminus ad quem* of the process of juridification of political power is the very idea of a constitution that a community of free and equal citizens gives itself. We must distinguish here between "constitution" and "state." A "state" is a complex of hierarchically organized capacities available for the exercise of political power or the implementation of political programs; a "constitution," by contrast, defines a horizontal association of citizens by laying down the fundamental rights that free and equal founders mutually grant each other. In this sense, the republican transformation of the

131

substance of state power by law is geared to the telos of a "constitution."

The completion of the process of constitutionalization sets the seal on the reversal of the initial situation in which law serves as an instrument of power. According to the self-understanding of the constitutional state, "all authority" springs from the autonomously (i.e. rationally) formed will of civil society (i.e. it "proceeds from the people"). Following the logic of the social contract, the starting point for the internal rationalization of governmental authority is a legally constituted but not yet constitutionally bound, and hence "substantive," power whose irrational core will be dissolved only in the democratic process of the fully established constitutional state. Against the background of this ideal scheme, we can now explain why the transition from the law of nations to cosmopolitan law can indeed be understood as a constitutionalization of international relations but not as a logical continuation of the evolution of the constitutional state leading from the national to a global state.

State organization vs. constitution

In view of their different starting points, the constitutionalization of international law and the domestication of untamed state power through the constitution cannot be understood in the same terms. International law, which in its classical form presents an inverted image of the state and the constitution, provides the starting point for a juridification of international relations that promotes peace. What is missing in classical international law is not an analogue of a constitution that founds an association of free and equal consociates under law, but rather a supranational power above competing states that would equip the international community with the executive and sanctioning powers required to implement and enforce its rules and decisions.

Classical international law is already a kind of constitution in the sense that it creates a legal community among parties with formally equal rights. To be sure, this international proto-constitution differs in essential respects from a republican constitution. It is composed of collective actors rather than individual persons, and it shapes and coordinates powers rather than founding new governmental authorities. Compared with a constitution in the strict sense, the international community of sovereign states lacks the binding force of reciprocal legal obligations. Only voluntary restrictions on sovereignty – above all, the renunciation of its core component, the right to go to war – can transform parties to treaties into members of a politically "constituted" community. Nevertheless, with the voluntary renunciation of aggression, members of a league of nations already accept a self-obligation that is more binding than the rules of customary law and international treaties even when there is no superordinate authority to enforce them.

A league of nations and the prohibition of war are logical extensions of a development connected with the *membership status* of the subjects of international law. At the beginning of the transformation process there is only a "weakly" constituted community of states (by comparison with the republican state), which must be supplemented at the supranational level by legislative and adjudicative bodies and by sanctioning powers if it is to become a community capable of taking political initiatives and executing joint decisions. In the course of the constitutionalization of international law, this priority of horizontal relations among member states over centralized practical competences points in an opposite evolutionary direction to that of the genealogy of the constitutional state. It proceeds from the non-hierarchical association of collective actors to the supra- and transnational organizations of a cosmopolitan order. Today this evolution finds expression in the three most imposing examples of international organizations, notwithstanding

133

the fact that they are quite diverse in function and structure. Whether they are called charters, agreements, or constitutions, the treaties which define the "constitution" of the United Nations, the World Trade Organization, or the European Union have one thing in common: they give the impression of a suit of clothes a couple of sizes too big waiting to be filled out by a stronger body of organizational law – in other words, by stronger transnational and supranational mandates for governance.

With such an empowerment of the loose international system of sovereign states, executive powers above the level of nation-states would complement the fragmentary proto-constitution of classical international law. The fact that this process runs counter to the foregoing process of taming state power by law can safeguard us from construing the constitutionalization of international law as simply a continuation of the development of the constitutional state at the global level. The democratic federal state writ large – the global state of nations or world republic – is the wrong model. No structural analogy exists between the constitution of a sovereign state that can determine what political competences it claims for itself (and hence possesses supreme constitutional authority), on the one hand, and the constitution of an inclusive world organization that is nevertheless restricted to a few, carefully circumscribed functions, on the other. A cursory reflection on the historical actors involved in both cases confirms the asymmetry between the evolution of state and cosmopolitan law. States that currently accept restrictions on their sovereignty for the sake of a regulated cooperation with other states are collective actors and have different motives and obligations from the revolutionaries who once founded constitutional states.

The initial situation of classical international law has left indelible traces in the Charter of the United Nations. It remains a community of states and peoples who mutually recognize each other's "sovereign equality" (Art. 2, Para. 1). On the other hand, in questions of international

security – and, meanwhile, also the promotion of human
rights – the world organization has acquired the authority
to intervene in the internal affairs of criminal governments or failing states. In these two policy domains, the
member states grant the UN Security Council the competence to protect the rights of citizens against their own
governments if necessary. Hence, it would be consistent
to describe the world organization as already a community
of "states and citizens." In a similar spirit, the Brussels
Convention presented its draft of the European constitution in the name of "the citizens and the States of Europe."
The reference to collective actors acknowledges the prominent position which they, as the driving subjects of the
development, will retain in a peaceful global legal order.
The reference to individuals, by contrast, draws attention
to the actual bearers of the status of world citizen.

Global domestic politics without a world government

The dual reference to collective and individual actors
marks a fundamental conceptual distinction between the
thoroughly individualistic legal order of a federal world
republic[37] and a politically constituted global society that
reserves institutions and procedures of global governance
for states at both the supra- and transnational levels.[38]
Within this framework, members of the community of
states are indeed obliged to act in concert, but they are
not relegated to mere parts of an overarching hierarchical
super-state. However, a constructive transformation in
the self-understanding of state actors whose sovereignty
is restricted and who are bound by consensual norms of
membership would not leave the mode of negotiating
power based on compromises hitherto dominant in international relations unaffected.

Taking one's orientation from currently existing structures, one can construe the political constitution of a
decentered world society as a multilevel system that for

good reasons lacks the character of a state *as a whole.*[39] On this conception, a suitably reformed world organization could perform the vital but clearly circumscribed functions of securing peace and promoting human rights at the *supranational* level in an effective and non-selective fashion without having to assume the state-like character of a world republic. At the intermediate, *transnational* level, the major powers would address the difficult problems of a global domestic politics which are no longer restricted to mere coordination but extend to promoting actively a rebalanced world order. They would have to cope with global economic and ecological problems within the framework of permanent conferences and negotiating forums. Apart from the US, at present there are no global players with a sufficiently representative mandate to negotiate and the necessary power to implement such policies. Nation-states in the various world regions would have to unite to form continental regimes on the model of an EU equipped with sufficient power to conduct an effective foreign policy of its own. International relations would continue to exist in a modified form at this intermediate level. Modification would already be required by the fact that, under an effective UN peace and security regime, even global players would be forbidden to resort to war as a legitimate means of resolving conflicts.

The multilevel system outlined would fulfill the peace and human rights goals of the UN Charter at the supranational level and address problems of global domestic politics through compromises among domesticated major powers at the transnational level. Here it is intended to serve merely as an illustration of a *conceptual* alternative to a world republic. A global domestic politics without a world government would be embedded within the framework of a world organization with the power to impose peace and implement human rights. This idea is intended to show, by way of example, that a "world republic" is not the only institutional form which the Kantian project could assume as an alternative to the surrogate of a league of nations. The requirements for a "cosmopolitan condition" understood in sufficiently abstract terms are not fulfilled by the model of a constitutional state projected onto a global scale alone.

The argument thus far supports the further claim that the model of a world republic implies not only a false representation of the sequence of the steps involved in the transition from international to cosmopolitan law but also a problematic account of its goal. For, in the globally extended constitutional state, state and constitution would also remain fused in one and the same institution. By contrast, the three essential elements actually combined in the historically successful form of the European nation-state – state apparatus, civic solidarity, and constitution – separate once we move beyond the nation-state. They will have to enter into a new configuration if the present-day, culturally divided, and highly stratified world society is to have the good fortune one day to acquire a political constitution. The state in its modern form is not a necessary precondition of a constitutional order. Supranational communities such as the UN or the EU do not have a monopoly on the legitimate use of force. They lack the core element of internal and external sovereignty of the modern administrative and tax-based state which provides the necessary backing for the rule of law. Yet they affirm the primacy of supranational law over national legal orders. In particular, the European law which is laid down in Brussels and Luxemburg is respected by the member states of the EU, even though it is they who hold the means of legitimate violence in reserve.

The thesis that capacities for collectively binding decisions "lag behind" the constitutionalized interactions of collective actors within international organizations – in other words, that there is a "gap" between "state" and "constitution" at the supranational level – raises the further question of whether "constitutions without a state" [*entstaatlichte Verfassungen*] could possibly conform to the familiar type of the republican constitution (which Kant had in mind). If not, then the "constitutionalization" of international law would take on a different meaning.

Taking the examples of the UN, the WTO, and the EU, Hauke Brunkhorst analyzes "legal orders without a state" with particular reference to the democratic deficit of a "rule of law without self-legislation."[40] In their function of containing and balancing divergent political powers, the constitutions of international organizations are reminiscent of paradigms of a pre-modern legal tradition. In early modern societies, political authorities were based on treaties between the crown or prince and the ruling estates (comprising the nobility, the Church, and the cities). This tradition gave rise to a concept of "constitution" geared toward setting limits to political domination through a distributive division of power. The idea of a mutual restriction and balancing of "ruling powers," already embodied in the old parliaments and city councils and tailored to collective representation, was developed further in modern theories of the state. The concept of a distributive "division of governmental authority" was reinterpreted in the individualistic terms of modern law – specifically, in terms of a conception of human rights – in English liberalism and in terms of a functional division of powers (between legislation, administration, and adjudication) in German constitutionalism. These constitute the sources of the "rule of law" and "Rechtsstaat" traditions, respectively.

Like the republican type of constitutionalism which Kant had in mind, these formal or informal liberal types aim at a juridification of political power. However, in the latter cases "juridification" means the domestication of power through the division and channeling of *existing* power relations. The revolutionary constitutions of republican pedigree, by contrast, overturn established powers in favor of a newly founded political authority grounded in the rationally formed will of the united citizenry.[41] Only this republican tradition invests the term "constitutionalization" with the meaning of rationalizing a quasi-natural, substantive state power. In opposition to the conservative tradition of public law, the declared aim here is that no residues of state power "behind the law" may remain untouched.

Supranational constitution and democratic legitimation

Halfway democratic procedures of legitimation have until now been institutionalized only at the level of the nation-state; they demand a form of civic solidarity that cannot be extended at will beyond the borders of the nation-state. For this reason alone, constitutions of the liberal type recommend themselves for political communities beyond states or continental regimes such as the EU.[42] They regulate the interplay among collective actors with the goal of setting mutual restrictions on their power; they direct the exercise of power governed by treaties into channels that conform with human rights; and they leave the tasks of applying and developing law to courts, though without being exposed directly to democratic inputs and controls. Here the "constitutionalization" of international law does not satisfy republican standards of democratic legitimation. Brun-Otto Bryde has the tradition of liberal constitutionalism in mind when he explicates the "constitutionalization" of international law by differentiating between the concept of a "constitutional order" and that of "state":

> Although a constitutional state [*Verfassungsstaat*] cannot exist at the international level, constitutionalism can; likewise, there cannot be a (global) *Rechtsstaat* but there can be a (worldwide) rule of law, there cannot be an international welfare state [*Sozialstaat*] but there can be (global) social justice. . . . The concept of "democracy" lacks this component [of state organization], but it is read in by translating "demos" by "sovereign people" [*Staatsvolk*] . . . whereas, in English, international political authority [*Herrschaftsgewalt*] can also proceed "from the people."[43]

139

However, this last inference is not self-evident. For, in liberal constitutionalism from Locke to Dworkin, the two sources of legitimation, human rights, and popular sovereignty, are not on a par with each other. The "rule of law" draws its legitimation from religious or metaphysical sources, ultimately from human rights, which are in turn grounded in the "natural order of things." However, it is difficult to defend this position in terms of postmetaphysical thinking. The republican conception of the constitution, by contrast, has the advantage that it bridges this gap in legitimation. At least the constructivist reading of discourse theory can explain how the principles of popular sovereignty and human rights mutually presuppose one another. On this reading, the legitimacy of the laws – including the basic laws on which the rule of law is founded – is anchored in the legitimating force of the at once deliberative and representative character of the procedures of democratic opinion- and will-formation which are institutionalized in law.[44] However, this interrelation between the rule of law and democracy would necessarily be dissolved if supranational constitutions were completely severed from the channels of democratic legitimation which are institutionalized within the constitutional state. Hence, liberal constitutions beyond the state, if they are to be anything more than a hegemonic legal façade, must remain tied at least indirectly to processes of legitimation within constitutional states.

Supranational constitutions rest at any rate on basic rights, legal principles, and criminal codes which are the product of prior learning processes and have been tried and tested within democratic nation-states. Thus, their normative substance evolved from constitutions of the republican type. This holds not only for the UN Charter and the Universal Declaration of Human Rights, but even for the treaties underlying GATT and the WTO. The regulation and arbitration of the WTO increasingly take into account the protection of human rights, in addition to the usual legal principles (such as non-discrimination,

reciprocity, solidarity, etc.).[45] To this extent, the constitutionalization of international law retains a derivative
status because it depends on "advances" of legitimation
from democratic constitutional states.

As Kant already recognized, the world organization will
finally be able to fulfill its tasks only when the inconspicu-
ous wording of the constitutional texts of all of the
member states has lost its merely nominal character.
Moreover, at the transnational level, organizations that
allow for an increasingly politicized mode of negotiation,
such as the WTO and other global economic institutions,[46] will acquire the ability to develop and conduct
something akin to a global domestic politics only when a
group of global players emerges in which the channels of
democratic legitimation are progressively extended
"upwards" from the level of the nation-state to the level
of continental regimes. The long overdue (but still by no
means imminent) "deepening" of EU institutions could
provide a model for this development.

If an effective constitutionalization of international law,
short of the creation of a global state, is to acquire the
legitimacy of a "cosmopolitan condition," it must satisfy
certain preconditions. Both at the level of the UN and of
transnational negotiation systems, it must receive indirect
"backing" from the kinds of democratic processes of
opinion- and will-formation that can only be fully institutionalized within constitutional states, regardless of
how complex federal states on a continental scale may
become. This weak form of constitutionalization beyond
the nation-state remains reliant on continual provisions
of legitimacy from within state-centered systems. Only
within states does the organizational part of the constitution secure citizens equal access to the politically binding
decisions of the government through institutionalized
publics, elections, parliaments, and other forms of participation. Only within constitutional states do administrative mechanisms exist to insure the equal inclusion of
citizens in the legislative process. Where these are lacking,

as in the case of the constitutions of international organizations, there is always the danger that the "dominant" interests will impose themselves in a hegemonic manner under the guise of impartial laws.

In the case of transnational negotiations between continental regimes, the need for legitimation may be met through a connection with the democratic infrastructure of their respective member states, assuming that the negotiation systems themselves ensure a fair balance of powers. At this level, major powers are more likely to fulfill expectations of fairness and cooperation the more they have learned to view themselves at the supranational level as members of a global community – and are so perceived by their own national constituencies from which they must derive their legitimation. But who is to say that the hegemonic law of the stronger (which is at present explicitly recognized by the veto power of the permanent members of the Security Council) is not entrenched, in turn, behind the façade of the world organization itself?

Hauke Brunkhorst's response to this question hints at the auxiliary role of a supportive global public sphere, though it can exercise only indirect influence: the spontaneous activity of a weak public sphere that does not have formal legal access to binding decisions at least makes possible a form of legitimation via a loose linkage of discussion and decision.[47] What concerns us here is not the empirical question of the actual strength of the legitimating pressure exercised by a global public on the policies of the world organization and the decisions of international courts, an influence generated by the media and news organizations and mobilized by social and political movements. What concerns us is, rather, the theoretical question of whether global communication in an informal public, without constitutionally institutionalized paths for translating communicative influence into political power, can secure a sufficient degree of integration for global society and whether it can confer a sufficient level of legitimacy on the decisions of the world organization.

Luckily, the level that must be achieved in order to satisfy these functional requirements is not unfeasibly high. If the international community limits itself to securing peace and protecting human rights, the requisite solidarity among world citizens need not reach the level of the implicit consensus on thick political value-orientations that is necessary for the familiar kind of civic solidarity among fellow-nationals. Consonance in reactions of moral outrage toward egregious human rights violations and manifest acts of aggression is sufficient. Such agreement in negative affective responses to perceived acts of mass criminality suffices for integrating an abstract community of world citizens. The clear negative duties of a universalistic morality of justice – the duty not to engage in wars of aggression and not to commit crimes against humanity – ultimately constitute the standard for the verdicts of international courts and the political decisions of the world organization. This basis for judgment provided by common cultural dispositions is slender but robust. It suffices for bundling the worldwide normative reactions into an agenda for the international community and it lends legitimating force to the voices of a global public whose attention is continually directed to specific issues by the media.

Trends which meet the Kantian project halfway

Kant understood permanent world peace as an implication of the complete constitutionalization of international relations. The same principles which previously took shape in the constitutions of republican states should also structure this cosmopolitan condition – it must accord everyone the same civil and human rights. In Kant, this idea of a cosmopolitan condition assumes concrete form in the constitution of a world republic. However, he is troubled by the tendency toward leveling, and even despotic, violence which seems to be endemic to the structure of a

THE KANTIAN PROJECT

world republic. This is why he falls back on the surrogate of a league of nations. If the global power monopoly of an all-conquering state of nations represents the only alternative to the coexistence of sovereign states, it seems better not to realize the idea of a cosmopolitan condition, which he nevertheless does not renounce, in the medium of coercive law. It should be realized instead in the weaker form of a voluntary association of peaceful republics. I have tried to show that the alternative which compels Kant to draw this conclusion does not exhaust the possibilities. If we conceive of the legal domestication of a belligerent international arena in sufficiently abstract terms and do not burden the idea with false analogies, a different path to the constitutionalization of international law, one opened up by liberal, federalist, and pluralist notions, seems at least conceptually possible.

International law has at any rate developed in this direction. This legal development was fostered in the context of an increasingly complex world society and a highly interdependent state system. It was a reaction to the challenges posed by military technology and security risks and, in particular, a response to the historical and moral experiences of the destruction of the European Jews and other horrendous mass crimes. Hence, it is not merely empty speculation to pursue the conceptual possibility of a multilevel political system that does not assume a state-like character as a whole – a system without a world government and a monopoly on force capable of securing peace and human rights at the supranational level and meeting the challenges of a world domestic politics at the transnational level. On the other hand, the paralyzing reality of a world gripped by violence offers ample reasons to ridicule these "dreams of a ghost-seer." It is also important to realize that the idea of a cosmopolitan condition, however normatively well founded, remains an empty, even deceptive, promise without a realistic assessment of the totality of accommodating trends in which it is embedded.

144

Kant also recognized this. Although he ascribed categorical moral validity to propositions such as "There shall be no war," he recognized the need for a philosophy of history whose heuristic aim was to lend the idea of the cosmopolitan condition empirical probability and plausibility. The accommodating trends he diagnosed at the time, however, were not just "accommodating." The peaceableness of democratic states, the pacifying effect of global trade and the critical function of the public sphere have proved with hindsight to rest on questionable assumptions. Although it is true that republics have generally behaved peacefully toward other republics, in other contexts they have been as energetic in their military pursuits as authoritarian states. In addition, the take-off of capitalism had disruptive effects not only during the age of imperialism. It produced a combination of modernization and a disruptive underdevelopment among the losers in the race to modernize. Moreover, a public sphere dominated by the electronic mass media is as much an instrument of manipulation and indoctrination (with private television often playing a deplorable vanguard role) as of information.

If we are to do justice to the enduring relevance of Kant's project, we must look beyond the prejudices associated with his historical horizon. Kant was also a child of his time and suffered from a certain color blindness:

- Kant's lifetime predated the new historical consciousness which achieved pre-eminence around 1800 and he remained insensitive to the perception of cultural differences which was already sharpened by early romanticism. Thus, although he recognized the divisive force of religious differences, he immediately qualified this with the remark that, although there may exist different sacred texts and historical creeds, "there can be only one single *religion* holding for all human beings and in all times."[48]

145

- Kant was so deeply influenced by an abstract notion of enlightenment that he was blind to the explosive force of nationalism. The highly influential political consciousness of ethnic membership in communities of shared language and descent was just awakening in Kant's time. During the nineteenth century, it would assume the form of national consciousness and not only cause calamities in Europe but also contribute to the imperialist expansion of the industrialized states.

- Kant shared with his contemporaries the "humanist" conviction of the superiority of European civilization and the white race. He failed to grasp the import of the selectivity of a particularistic international law that was tailored to a handful of privileged states and Christian nations. Only these nations recognized each other as possessing equal rights and they divided up the rest of the world among themselves into spheres of influence for colonial and missionary purposes.

- Kant was not yet aware of the importance of the fact that European international law remained embedded in a common Christian culture. Until World War I, the binding power of this background of implicitly shared values remained sufficiently strong to constrain the use of military force more or less within the boundaries of a legally disciplined conduct of war.

The provinciality of our historical consciousness vis-à-vis the future is not an objection to the universalistic program of Kantian moral and legal theory. Its blind spots betray a historically understandable selectivity in the *application* of the cognitive procedure of universalization and mutual perspective-taking which Kant associates with practical reason and which underlies the cosmopolitan transformation of international law.

Constitutionalization of International Law or Liberal Ethics of the Superpower

The history of international law in the light of current challenges

With the unearned epistemic privilege of later generations, we can survey a dialectical development of European international law spanning 200 years. The two world wars of the twentieth century and the end of the Cold War constitute junctures in this legal development, although the latter juncture does not yet exhibit such a clear pattern as the previous two. The two world wars were like watersheds in which new hopes arose as older ones subsided. The League of Nations and the United Nations are major, albeit precarious and reversible, achievements on the long, hard road to a political constitution for world society. The League of Nations collapsed as Japan invaded Manchuria, Italy annexed Abyssinia, and Hitler's aggressive military build-up brought initial successes with the Anschluss with Austria and the annexation of the Sudetenland. Since the Korean War, at the latest, the work of the United Nations has been hampered, if not brought to a complete stand-still, by a stand-off between the major powers and the stalemate within the Security Council.

The third juncture, the collapse of the Soviet Union, also inspires hopes for a new world order under the leadership of the world organization. With a series of humanitarian, peacekeeping and peace-enforcing interventions, with the establishment of war crimes tribunals and the prosecution of human rights violations, the United Nations seems to be finally capable of taking independent initiatives. At the same time, however, the setbacks are mounting, including the terrorist attacks interpreted by the US and its allies as a "declaration of war" against the West.

The developments which culminated in the invasion of Iraq by coalition troops in March 2003 have given rise to an ambiguous situation for which there are no parallels in the history of international law. On the one hand, a super-power that thought it could impose its will by military means as it saw fit, independently of Security Council resolutions, cited a right of self-defense. The most power-ful member of the United Nations disregarded its basic norm, the prohibition on violence. On the other hand, this clear violation of standing law did not destroy the world organization. On the contrary, the latter seems to be emerging from the conflict with its international authority enhanced.

Is this obscure situation an indication that progress in the constitutionalization of international law, after two calamitous setbacks, has nevertheless taken on a self-propelling dynamic? Or does it mark the beginning of the end of the whole project of juridifying international rela-tions? The diplomatic avoidance of an open conflict over the future of international law fosters a rhetorical grey area in which a perplexing fusion of a constitution for world society with the hegemonic law of a superpower – or the equally alarming prospect of a competition among hemispheres à la Carl Schmitt – could inconspicuously transpire. The propagandistic blurring of the clearly defined concept of "armed attack," coupled with euphe-mistic talk of "adapting" international law to accommo-date new risks, bode no good, especially when long overdue reforms are being used, in effect, as a pretext to suspend principles of international law.

The sanctioning of states whose governments provide a haven for, or actively support, the new international terror requires neither the erosion of the narrowly defined right of self-defense nor the suspension of key provisions of the Geneva Convention. Nor does effectively combating the new terror at the domestic level call for restrictions on basic rights that amount virtually to their destruction.[49] Of course, this specter could vanish with a change in administration in the United States. Nevertheless, the image of a superpower that uses its military, technological, and economic superiority to create a global order in accordance with its own religiously colored notions of good and evil and its geostrategic goals suggests a heuristically useful alternative, namely, one between a progressive constitutionalization of international law and its substitution by the liberal ethics of a superpower.

This issue points our attention to the history of international law (and of theories of international law) in a specific direction. Crucial for a proper understanding of the alternative and what underlies it is the concept of the juridification of international relations, in the sense of a transformation of international law into a cosmopolitan constitution. Kant ascribes an intrinsic capacity to *rationalize* political power to a law that is enacted and applied in an impartial manner. Without this premise, hegemonic unilateralism, which justifies momentous decisions by appeal to its own national values rather than in terms of established procedures, would assume a different meaning. It would no longer represent a conspicuous ethical *alternative* to international law but rather a recurrent imperial variant *within* international law.

On the latter conception, international law is restricted to coordinating relations between states. It is incapable of transforming the underlying power constellations and hence merely mirrors them in a different language. It can exercise its proper regulating, pacifying, and stabilizing functions only on the basis of *existing* power relations but it lacks the authority and the internal dynamic to empower a world organization to detect and sanction violations of international peace and human rights. On these alternative premises, international law merely provides a flexible medium for shifting constellations of power, rather than a crucible in which quasi-natural power relations could be dissolved. Accordingly, the ideal types of international law vary with existing constellations of power. At one end of the continuum is state-centered international law which reflects multilateral relations between sovereign states; at the other is the hegemonic law of an imperial power that withdraws from international law only in order, ultimately, to assimilate and incorporate it into its own national legal system.[50]

How should we decide between different conceptions of international law?[51] They not only conflict over the correct interpretation of the history of international law but are themselves so deeply embedded in political history that they influence its actual course. The relation between power and law is affected by the normative self-understanding of state actors, and hence is not a descriptively ascertainable constant. This fact, however, goes counter to the social-ontological reading according to which relations of power always provide the ultimate hermeneutic key to legal relations. The Kantian conception of international law, by contrast, allows for the possibility that a superpower, assuming it has a democratic constitution and acts with foresight and prudence, will not always instrumentalize international law for its own ends but can promote a project that ends up by tying its own hands. It may even be in its long-term interest not to deter emerging competing major powers with threats of pre-emptive strikes but to bind them in a timely fashion to the rules of a politically constituted international community.

The power of nationalism: Julius Fröbel before and after 1848

Even a cursory examination reveals the countervailing tendencies which have shaped the history of international law up to the present day. During the long nineteenth century, the prevailing belief that the political substance and world-historical vocation of sovereign nation-states could not be tamed by law overshadowed pacifist initiatives toward European unification: "The nation-state [*das Volk als Staat*] is the spirit in its substantial rationality and immediate actuality, and is therefore the absolute power on earth." With this slogan, Hegel, who discusses international law under the heading "*äußeres Staatsrecht*" still standard in German (in §§331–40 of his *Philosophy of Right*), takes aim at Kant's idea of a "perpetual peace through a confederation of states that adjudicates all disputes." Conflicts between sovereign states "can be settled only by war," because the unifying ethical backdrop of religious "agreement" is missing.[52] However, the tidal shift from humanistically enlightened to nationalistically biased liberalism was not fully completed in Germany until after the failed revolution of 1848.

The biography and work of Julius Fröbel, born in 1805 and the nephew of the educational reformer Friedrich Fröbel,[53] are exemplary in this regard. Fröbel studied in Jena with the Kantian Jakob Friedrich Fries and was influenced by Ludwig Feuerbach's critique of religion. He taught geography at the university in Zurich and came in contact with the Left Hegelian circle through Arnold Ruge before resigning from his teaching post for political reasons and becoming a publisher. Prior to participating in the constitutional convention in the Paulskirche in Frankfurt in 1848 as a member of the extreme left "Donnersberg" faction, he wrote a two-volume *System of Social Politics*, which appeared in 1847.[54] This "theory of constitutional law" inspired by Kant and Rousseau is outstanding in the originality of its reflections on the structure of the welfare state and the role of political parties in democracies, which point far beyond their time. Fröbel's understanding of deliberative politics makes him a forerunner of the procedural conception of the democratic constitutional state.[55]

Of particular interest in the present context, however, is the radicalization of the Kantian idea of the cosmopolitan condition in the context of the *Vormärz*.[56] Fröbel was already responding to the widespread debates inspired by Kant's essay on perpetual peace. He had to defend Kant's "call for justice and perpetual peace among states"[57] in a political and intellectual climate that, by comparison with the humanistic outlook of the eighteenth century, had changed as a result of the influence of Hegel and the historical school. Fröbel displays his wide-ranging cultural, historical, anthropological, ethnographic, and geographic knowledge concerning the differences between tribes, languages, and races because these conservative, "quasi-natural" elements of social and cultural life represent obstacles on the road to political liberation. Although the course of cultural development alternately "separates and joins" peoples, a tension remains between the roots of the ethnos and the will of the political nation. Switzerland served as an example for Fröbel: "Nations whose existence is based primarily on free association and federation are often held together only by external pressure until the components of the commonwealth have grown together to a certain extent."[58] Fröbel was passionately interested in the "ethical, free, genuinely political moment in the existence of nations," or what he called "federal fraternity based on free decisions."[59] From the beginning, he was looking beyond nation-states to a federation of states.

To be sure, as long as the nation persists in regarding itself as an end in itself, the consciousness of citizens in liberal states also retains a "limited patriotic character."[60] In the name of "self-determination, for which each person possesses his own standard,"[61] Fröbel categorically rejects such a substantialization of state and nation. Only equal respect for everybody and universal solidarity are worthy candidates for a "final end of culture." This ideal of humanity should take shape in a global federation of states that puts an end to war by overcoming the opposition between national and international politics, between state and international law. Fröbel paints the Kantian idea of the cosmopolitan condition in the striking colors of a "democratic federation of all human beings, of universal self-government of individuals joined together, who have an awareness of themselves as the autonomous residents, proprietors and cultivators of the earth."[62] In this, he takes his orientation from the federal system of the United States and, especially, the Swiss nation-state, rather than from the centralized French republic.

The idea of a federal world republic does not need the surrogate of a loose confederation of nations. Together with the right to go to war, the sovereignty of states that have been transformed into members of a larger union disappears as well as its obverse side, the principle of non-intervention, which Fröbel regards as "a sorry pretext in moments of weakness": "The question always remains whether an intervention is to be undertaken for the sake of freedom and culture or of egoism and coarseness."[63] Wars are permissible only "as revolutions," hence in the shape of liberation movements for promoting democracy and civil rights. To this end, parties to civil wars even deserve the support of intervening powers[64] and international courts should police the legality of such interventions.

Fröbel, the revolutionary, had to leave Germany in 1849 when a warrant was issued for his arrest. When the emigrant Fröbel returned after eight years in the United States, he had not only undergone an intellectual conversion to "Realpolitik," as witnessed by L. A. von Rochau; his personal assimilation of the harsh experience of a precarious immigrant existence was so attuned to the times that his writings became emblematic of the shift in political climate.[65] When he again published two volumes in 1861, fourteen years after the appearance of the *System of Social Politics*, this time under the title *Theory of Politics*,[66] he professes in the preface to have forsworn the "brazenness of the revolutionary spirit." He now follows Hegel and the historical school in viewing the state not as existing for the sake of its citizens but as an organic and sovereign ethical entity that is understood as an end in itself. Since states do not tolerate any authority above themselves, "power does not proceed from law, but law from power" in relations between states.[67] The state of nature in the international arena is destined to continue

153

forever: "Hence the universal state is an idea that completely contradicts ethical standards, not an ideal to which
reality can never attain but a pathology of the mind, an
error of ethical judgment."[68]

Kant, Woodrow Wilson, and the League of Nations

Fröbel was doubtlessly an academic outsider, but his
acute assessment of the Kantian project not only anticipated a fundamental tenet of Hegel's student Adolf
Lasson[69] but also gave expression to the background consensus among most of the constitutional lawyers in
Germany between 1871 and 1933.[70] Faced with the prominent "deniers" of international law from Erich Kaufmann
to Carl Schmitt, the influence of internationalists such as
Walther Schücking and Hans Kelsen remained marginal.
Nationalism and the preoccupation with the strong state
continue to this day to cast a long shadow over the liberal
impulses emanating from the profession of international
law in Western countries. Martti Koskenniemi devotes
two stimulating chapters of his impressive history of international law to the genuine, but ultimately equivocal,
endeavors of the jurists associated since the end of the
1860s with the Institut de droit international and the
Revue de droit international et de législation comparée. Many
of them would participate in the peace conferences at The
Hague. Until that time, and notwithstanding the Geneva
Convention of 1864, the *jus in bello* (i.e. the civilizing of
the conduct of war by restricting it to combatants, the
prohibition of treachery, the protection of civilians and the
wounded, the humane treatment of prisoners, the protection of cultural treasures, etc.) had not been brought under
universally binding regulations: "Indeed the laws of war
have perhaps never been studied with as much enthusiasm
before nor since the period between 1870 and 1914."[71]
These nationally minded liberals assumed that the
vocation of the international lawyer was to give voice

to the political conscience of humanity. The existence and independence of nation-states was a given; but only the European states belonged to a cultural domain in which the ideals of the Enlightenment, human rights, and humanitarian principles could be expected to meet with sympathy. Only the civilized societies appeared to them to be sufficiently mature to qualify as members of the international community of states with equal rights. The internationalists were not insensitive to the brutal aspects of colonialism but they also took the view that the Europeans had been burdened with the role of bringing civilization to all corners of the earth. From the perspective of the superiority of the white West, it appeared perfectly natural that the colonial powers should regulate their claims toward one another, but not their relations with their own colonies, by legal means. The existing differences in levels of cultures, and the resulting *mission civilisatrice*, supposedly explained why the universalism of international legal principles was compatible with the exclusionary logic inherent in the colonial project.

To be sure, the legal profession did not merely restrict itself to the dogmatic elaboration of international law; it also devoted itself with some success to issues of legal policy, in particular in the field of humanitarian international law. All the greater was the mental shock produced by the horrific trench warfare and mechanized slaughter of World War I (with tanks, poison gas, flame-throwers, etc.) among the peoples of Europe. The first "total" war rendered all attempts to subject military force to legal controls null and void. This contemptuous disavowal of the achievements of the Peace Conference at The Hague represented one side of the first major juncture in the history of classical international law; the other was the initiative of Woodrow Wilson, prompted by the shock of the war, to found the League of Nations. The long nineteenth century ended with an historical upheaval that prepared the way for the first, improbable steps toward a constitutionalization of international law.

155

The founding of the League of Nations placed the Kantian project on the political agenda for the first time. Not long afterwards, it also became the focus of major scholarly controversies among constitutional and international lawyers.[72] Only after the terror of World War I did Kant's idea have a concrete impact on the theory and politics of law. However, in an exhausted and decimated Europe the slogans of the peace movement found greater resonance among the public than among governments. It required the initiative of an American president who was well prepared for the task by his legal training to translate a philosophical idea into practice. Under the influence of the progressive internationalists, in particular, of the Women's Peace Party and the British radicals from the Union of Democratic Control,[73] Wilson had already developed the idea of a pacific league as the core of a post-war world order during the war, presenting it in a May 1916 address to the American League to Enforce Peace. Against the vacillation of the Allies, he could bring to bear the full weight of a major power that had for the first time made a decisive intervention in European conflicts.

Three months after an armistice had been signed through American mediation in November 1918, Wilson assumed the chairmanship of a commission charged with founding a league of nations. The commission came up with a draft charter after just eleven days of deliberations. In Germany, politically committed academics and intellectuals such as Karl Vorländer, Karl Kautsky, and Edward Spranger immediately recognized the influence of Kant's idea of a league or confederation of nations.[74] Although Wilson never appealed directly to Kant's work "Toward Perpetual Peace," numerous pieces of circumstantial evidence indicate that he must have been familiar with this source.[75] This intellectual debt to Kant is shown not only by the political goals but even more so by the composition and organization of the League of Nations. The prohibition of war, which overturns an essential feature of international law up to that point, represents a quantum leap in

156

the evolution of law. The first clause of Article 11 of the Charter of the League of Nations (comprising just 26 articles in total) stipulates that "Any war or threat of war, whether immediately affecting any of the Members of the League or not, is hereby declared a matter of concern to the whole League." No member of the League could remain neutral. This solemn commitment of the members was followed in 1928 by the absolute prohibition of war in Article 1 of the Kellogg-Briand Pact, to which American jurists once again made a decisive contribution.

Following the Kantian model, the League of Nations was supposed to achieve this goal through the voluntary self-obligation of peaceful sovereign and liberal states. Thus, the federation was supposed to combine state sovereignty with state solidarity based on the democratic self-determination of peoples organized as nation-states. Wilson clearly failed to appreciate the explosiveness of the principle of nationality which the Versailles Treaty made the basis of a wide-ranging territorial reorganization of Europe and the Middle East in 1919. The permanent members of the Assembly of the League were to be Great Britain, France, Italy, Japan, and the US (which, however, never ratified the Treaty). Wilson saw them as the vanguard of a new world order based on the rule of law and democratic self-determination. The substantive requirements for the acceptance of further members were also shaped by a liberal outlook. As in Kant, only the realization of the cosmopolitan condition would signal the definitive abolition of war: "What we seek is the reign of law, based on the consent of the governed, and sustained by the organized opinion of mankind."[76]

The provisions of Articles 8–17 of the Charter concerning the prevention of war establish a system of collective security on the basis of reciprocal obligations to come to each other's aid, restrictions on armaments, economic sanctions, and procedures of peaceful arbitration (by a board of arbitration, an international court or the Assembly of the League).[77] But without a legal codification of the new crime of "war of aggression," without an international court equipped with the requisite authority, and without a supranational authority willing and able to impose effective sanctions on belligerent states, the League had no means of effectively countering the aggression of the later "Axis" powers, Japan, Italy, and Germany (which had withdrawn from the League). It had long since succumbed to paralysis by the time fascist Germany began a world war that would wreak not just physical and material havoc on Europe. A breakdown in civilization far beyond the devastation of war rocked German culture and society to its moral core and posed a challenge to the rest of humanity.

The UN Charter: A "constitution for the international community"?

Henceforth, the harm to be averted was no longer only war that exploded all barriers and degenerated into total conflict. Now the danger was violence of a previously unimaginable level of savagery, the transgression of elementary and previously "inviolable" inhibitions, the wholesale trivialization and normalization of absolute evil. Confronted with this new form of evil, international law could no longer cling to the main premise underlying the prohibition on intervention. The mass crimes of the Nazi regime, which culminated in the destruction of the European Jews, and the state crimes committed by totalitarian regimes against their own populations undermined the presumption that the sovereign subjects of international law are immune from blame in principle. The monstrous crimes revealed the absurdity of ascribing moral and criminal indifference to state action. Governments, including officeholders, functionaries, and collaborators, could no longer enjoy immunity. Anticipating the definitions of crimes later integrated into international law, the Nuremberg and Tokyo military tribunals convicted the representatives, officials, and functionaries of the defeated regimes of war crimes, of the crime of preparing a war of aggression, and of crimes against humanity. This marked the beginning of the end of international law as a law of states. It also laid down the moral parameters for the protracted process through which the idea of establishing an international criminal court has gradually won acceptance.

Already during the war, Roosevelt and Churchill called in the 1941 Atlantic Charter for "the establishment of a wider and permanent system of general security." Following the Yalta Conference, the four victorious powers issued an invitation to a founding conference in San Francisco. The 51 founding members duly passed the Charter of the United Nations unanimously on April 25, 1945, after just two months of negotiations. Despite the enthusiasm displayed at the solemn founding ceremony, there was no agreement over whether the new international organization was supposed to go beyond the immediate goal of preventing war and initiate the transformation of international law into a cosmopolitan constitution. It is clear in retrospect that the vanguard of states represented in San Francisco had crossed the threshold to a constitutionalization of international law, provided that we understand the latter in the sense specified above: "The goal of constitutionalism . . . is to place limits on the peremptory power of the legislator – which, in the system of international law, is in the first instance the states which enact law – through superordinate legal principles, in particular human rights."[78]

In comparison with the shameful failure of the League of Nations in the interwar years, the second half of the short twentieth century was marked by an ironic contrast between major innovations in international law, on the one hand, and the stifling power constellation of the Cold War, on the other, which in practice thwarted the effectiveness of these achievements. We can observe a similar dialectical movement to that following World War I:

159

regression during the war, an innovatory thrust after the war, followed by a disappointment all the greater because of the new level attained. The paralysis which gripped the world body after the Korean War could be described in similar terms. However, this time there was a grinding deadlock at the political level, not a regression behind the level of law already reached. The United Nations remained intact as an organization and even gave the impression of business as usual. At any rate, it provided the framework for the continued production of norms.

Although the innovations in international law after 1945, which we will first examine, did not initially have much impact, they go beyond Kant's surrogate of a voluntary federation of independent republics. But rather than pointing toward a world republic equipped with a global monopoly of power, they point – this at least is their claim – toward a sanctioned regime of peace and human rights at the supranational level. This regime is supposed to provide the framework for a global domestic politics without a world government at the transnational level as global society becomes increasingly peaceful and liberal.

It is, of course, a matter of considerable controversy among legal scholars whether the UN Charter can be interpreted as a constitution.[79] I am not an expert in these matters, so I will simply highlight the three normative innovations which endow the Charter of the United Nations, in contrast to the Charter of the League of Nations, with prima facie features of a constitution. This is not to say that the Charter was from the beginning presented or intended as a global constitution. Like a picture puzzle, the wording of the Charter is open both to the conventional reading and to the constitutional interpretation. This is primarily due to three features: (a) the explicit connection of the purpose of securing peace with a politics of human rights; (b) the linkage of the prohibition on the use of violence with a realistic threat of prosecution and sanctions; and (c) the inclusive character of the world organization and the universal validity it claims for the law it enacts.

To be sure, only the historical change of 1989/90 has placed the question of whether the United Nations possesses a constitution that requires its member states to alter their political self-understanding on the agenda in a constructive fashion. Moreover, only since the recent Iraq War has this question had a polarizing effect both on the profession of international lawyers and on political public opinion. In my view, the UN Charter provides a framework in which we no longer *have* to understand the member states exclusively as subjects of international legal treaties. Together with their citizens, they can now understand themselves as the constitutional pillars of a politically constituted world society. Whether there are sufficiently strong motives for such a gestalt shift in the self-perception of the subjects of international law ultimately depends on the cultural and economic dynamics of the world society itself.

Three innovations in international law

I would like to discuss the three innovations of 1945 and 1948 already mentioned which go beyond the situation in 1919 and 1928 in an attempt to explain why this topic provides the backdrop for the "split of the West."

(1)   Kant understood the problem of abolishing war as one of creating a worldwide constitutional order. Although this project also provided the motivation for Woodrow Wilson's initiative to found a league of nations, the charter of the League itself does not draw a connection between world peace and a global constitution based on human rights. The development of international law remains a means to the end of averting war. All this changes with the UN Charter, which, in the second clause of the preamble, reaffirms "faith in fundamental human rights, in

161

the dignity and worth of the human person," and in Article 1, Paras. 1 and 3, links the political goals of global peace and international security with the promotion of "respect for human rights and for fundamental freedoms for all without distinction as to race, sex, language or religion" throughout the world. The Universal Declaration of Human Rights of December 10, 1948, which explicitly refers back to the statements from the preamble to the Charter, underscores this correlation.

With this, the international community commits itself to the global implementation of constitutional principles that had previously been realized only within nation-states.[80] The agenda of the United Nations has also gradually expanded beyond the goal of securing peace outlined in Article 1, Para. 1, to include the promotion and implementation of human rights. The General Assembly and the Security Council now interpret the crimes of "breaches of the peace," "acts of aggression," and "threats to the peace" broadly in accordance with their policy on human rights. Whereas the United Nations initially viewed itself as concerned only with interstate conflicts and military aggression, it increasingly responds to domestic conflicts, such as breakdowns of governmental authority, civil war, and egregious violations of human rights.

The Universal Declaration was supplemented in 1966 by the International Covenant on Civil and Political Rights and the International Covenant on Economic, Social, and Cultural Rights, as well as by a variety of anti-discrimination conventions. In the present context, the agencies for monitoring and reporting on violations of human rights operating on a global scale are particularly noteworthy. The UN High Commission for Human Rights is authorized to exert diplomatic pressure on the governments involved if need be. It also investigates petitions by individual citizens against violations of human rights by their own governments. Although it has no major practical effects at present, this institution of complaints by individuals is important in principle because it accords individual citizens recognition as immediate subjects of international law.[81] But the distance still to be traveled from state to cosmopolitan law may be judged from the fact that, although the convention on torture came into force in 1987 when ratified by 51 states, far fewer states have accepted its binding provisions regarding petitions by individuals.

(2)   The core of the Charter is the general prohibition on the use of violence, which cannot be overruled by an international treaty of any kind, e.g. one between members of a military alliance or a coalition such as NATO. The only exception is a narrowly defined right of self-defense that excludes idiosyncratic and restrictive reinterpretations. Thus, the principle of non-intervention does not hold for members who violate the general prohibition on the use of violence. The Charter makes provisions for sanctions in case of violations and, if necessary, the use of military force in the conduct of police operations.[82] Article 42 of the Charter marks the second and decisive step in the direction of a constitutionalization of international law. Whereas the Council of the League of Nations could only issue recommendations to its members concerning coercive measures, the Security Council can itself undertake the military measures it judges necessary. Article 43 even authorizes it to take command of the forces and logistical support that member states are obliged to make available to it.

This provision is inoperative, so there has never been a UN supreme command. Given that the UN is now involved in many urgent operations, it would be desirable if the larger member states were to maintain units in reserve for swift deployment in such cases. However, until now the Security Council has only commissioned or permitted member states to carry out its sanctions on its behalf. The Charter pays for the willingness of the major powers to cooperate by granting them veto rights that pose a major obstacle to the effectiveness of the Security Council. It was clear from the beginning that the fate of the world organization would be decided by its success in committing the major powers (and, currently, the sole remaining superpower) to a common practice. Only on this condition can one reasonably expect that participants will develop an awareness of acting as members of a community of states as they become accustomed to that practice. Interventionist powers become all the more aware of this role the more they have to confront the constructive task of nation-building, that is, the duty to reconstruct wrecked infrastructures and collapsed administrative authorities and to replenish exhausted social and moral resources.

The blueprint for governance without a world government can be read off from the by-now well-established practice of peacekeeping and peace-enforcing interventions – hence in the domain of external security which was the primary touchstone of state sovereignty on the classical conception. The world organization does not have the authority to define and extend its own spheres of competence, nor does it enjoy a monopoly on the legitimate use of force. The Security Council operates in carefully restricted policy fields under conditions of a decentralized monopoly of the means of legitimate violence that remains the preserve of individual states. Yet, in general, the authority of the Secretary General is sufficient to mobilize the resources needed to implement the resolutions of the Security Council among the members.

The sanctioning power of the Security Council also extends to establishing tribunals to prosecute crimes under international law (war crimes, preparations for wars of aggression, genocide, and other crimes against humanity). Members of government, officials, functionaries, and other associates are now personally liable for the acts they performed in the service of a criminal regime, a further proof that international law is no longer merely a law for states.

(3)   In contrast with the structure of a League of Nations composed of a vanguard of states that already possess liberal constitutions, the United Nations was designed to be inclusive from the beginning. Granted, all member states must accept the obligations imposed by the principles of the Charter and the human rights declarations; but from the first day states such as the Soviet Union and China were among the members of the Security Council accorded veto power. Today, the world organization, which has expanded to 193 members, comprises, in addition to liberal regimes, authoritarian and sometimes even despotic and criminal regimes. The price to be paid is a glaring contradiction between the professed principles of the world body and the human rights standards actually practiced by certain member states. This contradiction undermines valid norms and impairs the legitimacy of procedurally correct resolutions – when a country like Libya assumes the chairmanship of the human rights committee, for example. On the other hand, the principle of inclusive membership satisfies a necessary precondition for the international community's claim to transform international conflicts into domestic conflicts.

If all conflicts are to be resolved peacefully and channeled into civilized procedures – on an analogy with the judicial procedure of prosecution, due process, and punishment – then all states without exception must be treated as concerned members of the international community. The legal and political "unity of nations" presupposed in the Christian tradition since Francisco de Victoria and Francisco Suarez found institutional embodiment for the first time in the United Nations. Correspondingly, Article 103 of the Charter affirms the primacy of UN law over all other international treaties. The tendency toward a hierarchization of international law is also confirmed by Article 53 of the Vienna Convention on the Law of Treaties: "A peremptory norm of general international law is a norm accepted and recognized by the international community of States as a whole as a norm from which no derogation is permitted and which can be modified only by a subsequent norm of general international law having the same character."

Furthermore, the broad inclusion of the member states, which was a result of the post-1945 process of decolonization, finally shattered the framework of European international law and ended the West's monopoly on interpretation. During the nineteenth century, non-European countries such as the US, Japan, and the Ottoman Empire were accepted as the subjects of international law. However, only within the framework of the UN did awareness of the cultural and religious pluralism of an increasingly complex world society transform the concept of international law itself. As a result of increased sensitivity to racial, ethnic, and religious differences, the members of the General Assembly have extended mutual perspective-taking into domains that remained beyond Kant's purview (and also that of Woodrow Wilson, who was anything but progressive in dealing with the race problem in the United States). The catalogues of human rights and the Declaration on the Elimination of all Forms of Racial Discrimination demonstrate this. With the Vienna Conference on Human Rights, the United Nations confirmed the need for an intercultural dialogue on disagreements over the interpretation of its own principles.[83]

The two faces of the Cold War

The quantum leap in the development of international law following World War II produced institutions that led an existence largely shielded from the political realities for many decades. The Security Council agreed once again on military measures during the Korean conflict, though only in the form of a call to collective self-defense. During the Cold War, it did not manage to continue the practice of the war crimes tribunals of Nuremberg and

Tokyo which had been overshadowed by the suspicion of "victor's justice." Under the conditions of the mutual nuclear threats of NATO and the Warsaw Pact, the methodological differentiations between legal and political science, international law and international order, lost their purely analytical character. In the bipolar world itself, a chasm opened up between norms and facts – facts to which the norms could not be applied. The discourse of human rights degenerated into mere rhetoric, while the "realist school" in international relations theory increasingly influenced policy both in Washington and in Moscow.

The constellation formed by the Cold War and the impotence of international law could not fail to favor a theory that based the apparently well-founded conclusion that international institutions are chronically ineffectual on a straightforward anthropological premise.[84] In the view of Hans Morgenthau, the founder of the realist school, the incessant drive for power is rooted in human nature.[85] The law-governed regularities of international relations, dominated exclusively by the interest in power and its accumulation, are also supposed to be rooted in this invariant anthropological disposition. In this arena, legal provisions can be nothing other than reflections of unstable and shifting interest constellations among powers. Moral condemnations and justifications intended to penalize opponents are counterproductive because they merely intensify conflicts, which are best managed by rational, sober, game-theoretical considerations.[86]

On the other hand, the uncoupling of an ideological rhetoric of human rights from power calculations also explains why the United Nations continued to produce norms freed from the pressure of events. The political contours of a future global order remained vague on both sides. Neither "realists" nor "idealists" had any reason to reflect seriously on a political constitution for world society. The former did not even believe in it, whereas the latter had to view it as lying in the distant future.

Paul W. Kahn, who establishes an interesting connection between the realism of the Morgenthau school and the jurisprudential neoliberalism of the 1990s, recognizes the enduring relevance of this ambiguity of the post-war period. The complementary reluctance of realists and idealists, both of whom neglected to clarify the notion of a new world order, though for conflicting reasons, weighs even upon the situation following 1989:

> We can speak of [the Cold War] as an age of tremendous growth in human rights law, but we must simultaneously recognize this as an age of gross violations of human rights. Should we look to the genocide convention or the outbreak of genocidal behavior to characterize this age? . . . Should we look to the prohibition on the use of force – the central tenet of the UN order – or the millions of dead in numerous wars that characterized this same period? It was an age that promised constraints on the state through law yet reached a kind of apotheosis of the state in adoption of policies of mutually assured destruction. The realist could be dismissive of international law, while the idealist could describe all of the recalcitrant fact[s] as a kind of rearguard action by outmoded political institutions. Similarly, the triumph of the West at the conclusion of the Cold War resists easy characterization. . . . Was it our ideas or our military-technological edge, our conception of rights or our economic power that triumphed? Of course, it was both, but that just means that the ambiguity that infused the post-World War II compromise had not been resolved even with the end of the Cold War.[87]

The unclarified ambiguity of the post-war period remains problematic to this day. It took the recent Iraq War to alert the West to the fact that it lacked a shared perspective. At most, the neoliberals in the 1990s were inspired by swift economic globalization to dream of the withering away of the state. The war rhetoric emanating from the White House and the return of a Hobbesian security regime represented a rude awakening from this dream. In the interim, a number of possible scenarios for

THE CONSTITUTIONALIZATION OF INTERNATIONAL LAW

a future global order have emerged. Alongside the neoliberal and the Kantian projects, the hegemonic vision of the American neoconservatives has taken on clear contours and, by way of reaction, has provoked a revival of a culturalist variant on the theory of hemispheres on the Left. I will return to this theme in the closing section of this chapter. But first, I would like to depict the current situation in broad outlines.

The ambivalent 1990s

Once the competition between social systems and the deadlock in the Security Council had been overcome, the UN – until then a "fleet in being" – would become an important forum of global politics. Beginning with the first Iraq War, between 1990 and 1994 alone the Security Council authorized economic sanctions and peacekeeping interventions in eight instances and military interventions in five further cases. It has proceeded somewhat more cautiously since the setbacks in Bosnia and Somalia; aside from arms embargoes and economic sanctions, there have been UN authorized missions in Zaire, Albania, the Central African Republic, Sierra Leone, Kosovo, East Timor, the Congo, and Afghanistan. The global political role of the Security Council also became clear in the two cases in which it withheld permission for military interventions, namely, the NATO intervention in Kosovo and the invasion of Iraq by American and British troops. In the former case, there were good reasons to regret the indecisiveness of the Security Council;[88] in the latter, the Security Council further enhanced the reputation the United Nations had acquired by rejecting an undertaking that was manifestly contrary to international law and pointedly refusing to grant retrospective legitimacy to the military facts on the ground.

Three circumstances underscore the increased political authority of the United Nations. The Security Council not only becomes involved in international conflicts but also intervenes in *conflicts within states*, be it, (a) in response to violence caused by civil wars or breakdowns in government (as in the former Yugoslavia, Libya, Angola, Burundi, Albania, the Central African Republic, and East Timor); or (b) in response to gross violations of human rights or ethnic cleansing (as in Rhodesia and South Africa, Northern Iraq, Somalia, Rwanda, and Zaire); or (c) in order to promote democracy (as in Haiti or Sierra Leone).[89] In addition, the Security Council drew on the tradition of Nuremberg and Tokyo in establishing *war crimes tribunals* for the massacres in Rwanda and the former Yugoslavia.

Finally, the dubious concept of so-called "rogue states"[90] (John Rawls uses the more neutral term "outlaw states") marks not only the intrusion of a fundamentalistic outlook into the rhetoric of the leading Western power, but also a concretization of the practice of recognition in international law. In international affairs, states that violate the security or human rights standards of the United Nations are increasingly stigmatized. The regular reports of globally active monitoring organizations, such as Human Rights Watch and Amnesty International, contribute essentially to such states losing their legitimacy.[91] A combination of external threats and persuasion and internal opposition has succeeded in winning concessions from certain governments (such as Indonesia, Morocco, and Libya).

On the other hand, these advances are counterbalanced by sobering facts. The world organization has a weak financial base. In many interventions, it encounters the delaying tactics of uncooperative governments that continue to enjoy exclusive control over military resources and depend, in turn, on the support of their national publics. The intervention in the civil war in Somalia was a failure in part because the American government withdrew its troops in response to the negative mood of its own population. Even worse than such failed interventions are interventions that never take place, or take place

170

too late, as in Iraqi Kurdistan, Angola, the Congo, Nigeria, Sri Lanka, and, it must also be said, Afghanistan. Aside from the fact that members of the Security Council with veto power such as Russia and China can thwart any intervention in their "internal affairs," the African continent suffers under the selective perception and asymmetrical evaluation of humanitarian catastrophes.

The commander of the UN troops stationed in Rwanda alerted the relevant branch of the UN to the fact that a mass murder was imminent as early as January 1994. The massacre duly began on April 7 and in the course of the next three months claimed 800,000 lives, mainly among the Tutsi minority. The UN vacillated too long over a military intervention that it was obligated to undertake under the Genocide Convention of 1948. Such shameful selectivity on the part of the Security Council in acknowledging and addressing specific cases reveals the primacy still enjoyed by national interests over the global obligations of the international community. The reckless disregard for obligations applies especially to the West, which is today confronted with the negative impacts of a failed process of decolonialization in addition to the long-term consequences of its colonial history, not to mention the effects of processes of economic globalization that are insufficiently counterbalanced by political institutions.[92]

The United Nations is increasingly encountering a new type of violence in both of its main areas of competence, i.e., threats to international security and egregious human rights violations. In response to the challenges posed by criminal states, the UN can mobilize military forces from member states should the need arise. To be sure, governments still play a dangerous role in the clandestine acquisition and illegal manufacture of weapons of mass destruction and governments continue to be involved in ethnic cleansing and terrorist attacks. However, threats emanating from criminal states are increasingly overshadowed by the risks generated by privatized violence no longer tied to the armed forces of a functioning state. In contrast with classical civil wars between ideological opponents, the "new wars" frequently result from "failing states," that is, from the collapse of a state authority that fragments into an unholy mixture of ethnonationalism, tribal feuds, international criminality, and civil war terrorism.[93]

A different matter again is the current danger of a global terrorism that draws its energy from religious fundamentalism and is all the more difficult to combat because it is deterritorialized.[94] What is new is not the terroristic intent, nor even the type of attack (notwithstanding the symbolic significance of the Twin Towers). The novelty lies in the specific motivation, and even more so in the logistics, of this form of privatized violence which operates globally but is only weakly networked. The "success" achieved by the terrorists in their own eyes since September 11, 2001 can be explained by a variety of factors, two of which merit particular attention: first, the disproportionate resonance with which the terror meets in a highly complex society suddenly aware of its own vulnerability, and, second, the incommensurate reaction of a highly armed superpower that deploys the technological potential of its army against non-state networks. The terrorists' calculation aims at a "success" in direct proportion to the anticipated "military and diplomatic, domestic-legal and social-psychological consequences of the attacks."[95]

The weaknesses of a UN in urgent need of reform are manifest. But the new types of privatized violence which make increasingly frequent and urgent demands on the conflict-solving and constructive ordering accomplishments of the international community are merely the most pressing symptoms of the dissolution of the national constellation and the transition to a postnational constellation. These trends, which are currently capturing attention under the heading of globalization, do not only run counter to the Kantian project of a cosmopolitan order; they also meet it halfway. Globalization also provides a supportive context for the aspiration to a cosmopolitan condition, one that mitigates the initial appearance of invincibility of the forces opposed to a political constitution for global society.

The reform agenda

The reform agenda for the core domains of the UN is not especially controversial. It follows as a matter of course from the record of the successes and failures of the existing institutions:

- Given its wide-ranging competences, the composition and mode of decision-making of the Security Council must be brought into harmony with the new geopolitical situation, with the aim of strengthening its capacity for action and of assuring adequate representation for the major powers and whole continents, while also taking account of the legitimate interests of a super-power that must be kept integrated into the world organization.
- The Security Council must be able to operate independently of national interests in its choice of agenda and its resolutions. It must bind itself to actionable rules that lay down, in general terms, when the UN is authorized *and obligated* to take up a case.[96]
- The executive is hampered by inadequate financing[97] and by restrictions on how it can access the requisite resources of the member states. Given the decentralized monopolies on the use of violence enjoyed by individual states, the executive must be reinforced to a point where it can guarantee the effective implementation of resolutions of the Security Council.
- The International Court of Justice has now been augmented by an International Criminal Court (though the latter has not yet won broad recognition). The adjudicative practice of such a Court will promote the

173

requisite definition and codification of the loosely defined crimes laid down in international law. Until now, the *jus in bello* has not been developed into a law of intervention that would protect affected populations against UN operations in a way analogous to the protection enjoyed by private citizens against domestic police operations. (In this connection, advances in military technology might even for once facilitate the transformation of wars into police operations, namely with the development of so-called precision weapons.)

- The legislative decisions of the Security Council and the General Assembly require a more robust, if indirect, form of legitimation from a well-informed global public opinion. In addition to other options, the continuous presence of non-governmental organizations (with observer status in UN institutions and reporting duties in national parliaments) also plays an important role in this connection.
- But this weak legitimation will suffice for the activity of the world organization only if the latter restricts itself to the most elementary tasks of securing peace and human rights on a global scale.

We can take it for granted that these basic rights are accepted as valid worldwide and that the judicial oversight of the enforcement of law for its part follows rules that are recognized as legitimate. In both respects, the supranational procedures of a politically constituted world society would build on legal principles that have long since proved themselves within individual constitutional states. At the supranational level, the enforcement of established law takes precedence over the constructive task of legislation and policy-making, both of which, on account of the greater scope for decision, demand a higher degree of legitimation, and hence more effectively institutionalized forms of citizen participation. Many of the more than 60 special and sub-organizations within the UN family, which we have not thus far discussed, are concerned with such political tasks.

Of course, some of these organizations, such as the International Atomic Energy Agency in its role of monitoring the production and proliferation of weapons of mass destruction, function as executive organs of the Security Council. Other organizations, such as the Universal Postal Union and the International Telecommunication Union, which date back to the nineteenth century, fulfill coordination functions in technical areas. However, the mandates of organizations such as the World Bank, the International Monetary Fund, and above all the World Trade Organization extend to political decisions with an immediate impact on the global economy. The key to understanding this complex collection of loosely connected international organizations in the narrower and wider penumbra of the UN lies in the emergence of a world society, chiefly as a result of the globalization of markets and communication networks.

We must focus on these processes when we ask why states allow themselves to be drawn into transnational networks and even join supranational alliances, and when we want to explain why they might one day even meet the challenge to reform the world organization in an effective way. For the globalization of economy and society has condensed the context in which Kant already embedded his idea of a cosmopolitan condition into a postnational constellation. By "globalization" is meant the cumulative processes of a worldwide expansion of trade and production, commodity and financial markets, fashions, the media and computer programs, news and communications networks, transportation systems and flows of migration, the risks generated by large-scale technology, environmental damage and epidemics, as well as organized crime and terrorism. These processes enmesh nation-states in the dependencies of an increasingly interconnected world society whose functional differentiation effortlessly bypasses territorial boundaries.

The postnational constellation

These systemic processes are altering the social parameters for the *de facto* independence of sovereign states.[98] Nation-states can no longer secure the boundaries of their own territories, the vital necessities of their populations, and the material preconditions for the reproduction of their societies by their own efforts. In spatial, social, and material respects, nation-states encumber each other with the external effects of decisions that impinge on third parties who had no say in the decision-making process. Hence, states cannot escape the need for regulation and coordination in the expanding horizon of a world society that is increasingly self-programming, even at the cultural level. States remain the most important actors and the final arbiters on the global political stage. Admittedly, they have to share this arena with global players of a different kind, such as multinational corporations and non-governmental organizations, which pursue their own agendas in the media of money or influence. However, only states can draw on the resources of law and legitimate power. Even if non-governmental actors can satisfy the initial regulatory needs of cross-border functional systems through private forms of legislation (e.g. corporations that institutionalize market relations with the aid of international law firms),[99] these regulations will not count as "law" if they are not implemented by nation-states, or at least by agencies of politically constituted international organizations.

Although nation-states are losing certain competences (for example, the ability to tax domestic companies that operate internationally), they are simultaneously gaining latitude for a new sort of political influence.[100] The quicker they learn to direct their interests into the new channels of "governance without government," the sooner they will be able to replace the traditional forms of diplomatic pressure and military force with the exercise of "soft" power.

The best indicator for the transformations of international relations is the blurring of boundaries between domestic and foreign policy.

In this way, then, the postnational constellation meets the constitutionalization of international law halfway. The everyday experience of growing interdependencies in an increasingly complex global society also imperceptibly alters the self-image of nation-states and their citizens. Actors who previously made independent decisions learn new roles, be it that of participants in transnational networks who succumb to technical pressures to cooperate, or that of members of international organizations who accept obligations as a result of normative expectations and the pressure to compromise. In addition, we should not underestimate the capacity of international discourses to transform mentalities under the pressure to adapt to the new legal construction of the international community. Through participation in controversies over the application of new laws, norms that are merely verbally acknowledged by officials and citizens gradually become internalized. In this way, nation-states learn to regard themselves at the same time as members of larger political communities.[101]

As we in the European Union have discovered, however, this flexibility runs up against the limits of existing forms of solidarity once nation-states unite to form continental regimes. For these regimes unavoidably take on characteristics of a state as soon as they develop into global players. Moreover, if the chains of democratic legitimation are not to break, civic solidarity must extend across former national borders within the enlarged communities.[102] As everywhere in modern states, solidarity, even in the abstract, legally constituted form of civic solidarity, is a scarce resource. It is all the more important that the unification of Europe should succeed, since this experiment could serve as a model for other regions of the world. In Asia, Latin America, Africa, and the Arab world, processes of regional political integration are still in their infancy. If these alliances do not take on a more concrete and at the same time democratic form, the obvious lack of collective actors capable of negotiating and implementing transnational compromises will remain acute.

International organizations operate more or less well at this intermediate level as long as they perform coordinating functions. However, they fail in tasks of global regulation in the fields of energy and environmental policy and in financial and economic policy. Either there is a lack of political will or the West imposes law hegemonically in its own interest. David Held goes beyond merely highlighting the unequal distribution of life chances in a world in which 1.2 billion human beings live on less than one dollar per day, in which 20 percent consume more than 80 percent of global income and in which all other indicators of "human development" point to similar disparities:

> [W]hile free trade is an admirable objective for progressives in principle, it cannot be pursued without attention to the poorest in the least well-off countries who are extremely vulnerable to the initial phasing in of external market integration . . . [T]his will mean that development policies must be directed to ensure the sequencing of global market integration, particularly of capital markets, long-term investment in health care, human capital and physical infrastructure and the development of transparent, accountable political institutions. . . . But what is striking is that this range of policies has all too often not been pursued.[103]

The pressure of problems generated by an increasingly globalized society will sharpen the sensitivity to the growing need for regulation and fair policies at the transnational level (i.e. the intermediate level between nation-states and the world organization). At present, we lack the actors and negotiation procedures that could initiate such a global domestic politics. Realistically speaking, we can only envisage a politically constituted world society as a multilevel system that would remain incomplete without this intermediate level.

Alternative Visions of a New Global Order

A U-turn in US policy on international law after September 11?

The United States does not need to develop the capacity to operate at the global level – it already has it. As the only global player of its kind, the superpower can escape international legal obligations without fear of sanction. On the other hand, the project of a cosmopolitan order is doomed to failure without American support, indeed American leadership. The US must decide whether it should abide by international game rules or whether it should marginalize and instrumentalize international law and take things into its own hands. Already the decision of the Bush administration to refuse to recognize the International Criminal Court, alongside such countries as China, Yemen, Qatar, Libya, and Saddam's Iraq, and, in particular, its unilaterally forced-through invasion of Iraq and the concurrent attempts to discredit the United Nations, seem to signal a U-turn in American policy on international law. Of course, one can properly speak of a "U-turn" only if the US government had pursued a different course during the 1990s.

Even during this period, American policy on international law did not exhibit unswerving commitment to the internationalism of the early post-war years. As in the period following 1945, the US exhibited a remarkable degree of activism in the field of international law following the end of the Cold War. However, it was pursuing a double agenda. On the one hand, it threw its weight behind the liberalization of trade relations and financial markets, the expansion of GATT to the World Trade Organization, the protection of intellectual

179

property, and so forth. Without American initiatives, important innovations in other areas – such as the conventions on landmines and chemical weapons, the expansion of the treaty on the non-proliferation of nuclear weapons and even the Rome Statute for the International Criminal Court – would never have got off the ground. On the other hand, the American government either failed to ratify many treaties or rejected them out of hand, in particular, treaties in the areas of arms control, human rights, the prosecution of international crimes, and environmental protection. Examples include the convention on landmines and the nuclear test-ban treaty, the right of individuals to submit petitions to the UN Commission on Human Rights, the conventions on the law of the seas and the protection of endangered species and – concurrent with the collapse of the convention on biological weapons and the unilateral withdrawal from the ABM Treaty – the Kyoto Protocol and the Statute of the ICC. As a general rule, the USA ratified a considerably smaller proportion of the multilateral treaties passed by the General Assembly than did the other G7 countries.[104]

These examples seem to conform to the classical pattern of behavior of an imperial power that rejects international legal norms because they limit its scope for action.[105] Even the humanitarian interventions and the military deployments authorized – or, as in the case of the NATO Kosovo mission, retrospectively legitimated – by the Security Council do not speak for an unambiguous reinforcement of the UN. Once the superpower exploits the instruments of international legal multilateralism to promote its own interests, this development acquires a thoroughly ambivalent significance.[106] What from one angle appears to be progress on the path to the constitutionalization of international law, from another appears to be the successful imposition of imperial law.

Some authors would even like to read into the undeniably internationalist orientation of US policy on international law following 1945 the hegemonic attempt to expand its own legal system to a global scale – in other words, the attempt to replace international law with national law: "America promoted internationalism and multilateralism for the rest of the world, not for itself."[107] On this view, even the decidedly internationalist policies of Roosevelt and Wilson, both of whom entered into overseas alliances in opposition to the "America First Doctrine" and became involved in the power politics of America's European allies, are brought into proximity with George W. Bush's unilateralism. Bush seems to be the heir to both traditions: the idealism of the American mission and the realism of a Jefferson who warned against "entangling alliances." With a clear conscience, this President unilaterally imposes US national territorial and security interests in the name of the ethos of a new liberal global order that he regards as a reflection of American values. However, once the globalization of a particular ethos has replaced the law of the international community, whatever is then dressed up as international law is in fact imperial law.

The evidence on which some critical readings of American policy on international law since 1989/90 are based does not support this kind of over-hasty imputation of false continuities. The highly asymmetrical distribution of power in a global society marked by cultural differences and asynchronous forms of life, which is nevertheless becoming increasingly integrated under systemic pressures, represents a highly ambivalent constellation; hence, it would be odd if one could read off unambiguous intentions from the political decisions of a superpower operating under such conditions. Let us assume counterfactually that the superpower sees itself at the forefront of the constitutionalization of international law, that it wants to promote the reform of the UN and to pursue the goal of a politically constituted cosmopolitan society, mindful of its own interests but respecting established procedures. Even in this ideal case it would not be possible to determine directly whether asymmetries of power were still lurking behind specific hegemonic acts that promote the juridification of international relations. Hegemonic law is still law. A well-intentioned and far-sighted hegemon of this sort would be the darling of future historians who lived to witness the happy outcome of the difficult experiment. Contemporaries living through the process without the benefit of the hindsight enjoyed by later generations, by contrast, will experience this history as involving an ambivalent mixture of attempts at constitutionalization of international law on the one hand and its instrumentalization on the other.

Of course, even contemporaries can recognize a clearcut U-turn from an internationalist to an imperialist strategy. Those who locate the unilateralism of the Bush administration within a historical pattern of consistent imperialistic behavior trivialize the importance of what is in fact an abrupt reversal in policy. In September 2002, the US President announced a new security doctrine in which he reserves a self-defined discretionary right to launch pre-emptive strikes. In his State of the Union address on January 28, 2003, he solemnly declared that if the Security Council did not ultimately agree to military action against Iraq, however this was justified, he would, if necessary, act contrary to the prohibition on the use of violence of the UN Charter ("The course of this nation does not depend on the decisions of others"). Taken together, these two actions are alarming indicators of an unprecedented rupture with a legal tradition that no previous American government had ever explicitly questioned. They express contempt for one of the greatest achievements of human civilization. The words and actions of this President do not admit any other conclusion than that he wants to *replace* the civilizing force of universalistic legal procedures with the particular American ethos armed with a claim to universality.

The weaknesses of hegemonic liberalism

This brings me back to my initial question: in view of the challenges we are currently facing, does the inefficiency of the United Nations, its selective perception and temporary inability to act, provide sufficient reasons to break with the premises of the Kantian project? Since the end of the Cold War, a unipolar global order has emerged in which a single military, economic, and technological superpower enjoys unrivaled supremacy. This fact is indifferent from a normative point of view. Only if one interprets it as generating a prejudice in favor of a *pax Americana* based on power instead of law does it demand a normative response. For the happy circumstance that the superpower is also the oldest democracy on earth could inspire a completely different approach from that of hegemonic unilateralism – one oriented to the global expansion of democracy and human rights. In spite of an abstract agreement in their goals, the hegemonic liberal vision differs from the Kantian project of promoting a cosmopolitan order both in the path that is supposed to lead to this goal and the concrete form the goal is supposed to take.

As regards the path, an ethically grounded unilateralism is no longer bound by established procedures in international law. Moreover, with regard to the concrete form of the new global order, hegemonic liberalism does not aim at a law-governed, politically constituted world society, but at an international order of formally independent liberal states. The latter would operate under the protection of a peace-securing superpower and obey the imperatives of a completely liberalized global market. On this model, the peace would not be secured by law but by imperial power, and the world society would be integrated, not through the political relations among world citizens, but through systemic, and ultimately market, relations. However, neither empirical nor normative considerations support this vision.

The undeniably acute danger of international terrorism cannot be combated effectively with the classical instruments of war between states nor, consequently, by the military superiority of a unilaterally acting superpower. Only the effective coordination of intelligence services, police forces, and criminal justice procedures will strike at the logistics of the adversary; and only the combination of social modernization with self-critical dialogue between cultures will reach the roots of terrorism. These means are more readily available to a horizontally juridified international community that is legally obligated to cooperate than to the unilateralism of a major power that disregards international law. The image of a unipolar world accurately mirrors the existing asymmetrical distribution of political power. However, it is misleading because the complexity of a world society that is not just economically decentered can no longer be mastered from a center. Conflicts between cultures and major religions can no more be controlled exclusively by military means than crises on world markets can be by political means.

Hegemonic liberalism is not supported by normative reasons either. Even if we assume a best-case scenario and ascribe the purest of motives and most intelligent policies to the hegemonic power, the "well-intentioned hegemon" will nevertheless encounter insuperable cognitive obstacles. A government that must decide on issues of self-defense, humanitarian interventions, or international tribunals on its own can act with as much consideration as it likes; in the unavoidable process of weighing goods it can never be sure whether it is really distinguishing its own national interests from the universalizable interests that all the other nations could share. This inability is a function of the logic of practical discourses; it is not a matter of good or bad will. One can only test a unilateral anticipation of what would be rationally acceptable to all sides by submitting the presumptively

184

unbiased proposal to a discursive procedure of opinion-
and will-formation.

"Discursive" procedures make egalitarian decisions
dependent on prior argumentation (only justified decisions are accepted); they are inclusive (all affected parties
can participate); and they compel the participants to
adopt each other's perspectives (a fair assessment of all
affected interests is possible). This is the cognitive meaning
of an impartial decision-making process. Judged by this
standard, the ethical justification of a unilateral undertaking by appeal to the presumptively universal values of
one's own political culture must remain fundamentally
biased.[108]

This defect cannot be made good by the fact that the
hegemonic power has a democratic internal constitution.
For its citizens confront the same cognitive dilemma as
their government. The citizens of one political community cannot anticipate the outcome of the interpretation
and application of supposedly universal values and principles made by the citizens of another political community from their local perspective and in their own cultural
context. In another respect, however, the fact that the
superpower has a liberal constitution is indeed important.
Citizens of a democratic political community sooner or
later become aware of cognitive dissonances if universalistic claims cannot be squared with the particularistic
character of the obvious driving interests.

The neoliberal and post-Marxist approaches

However, hegemonic liberalism is not the only alternative
to the Kantian project. In conclusion, I would like to
examine three further visions that are currently being
advanced:

- the neoliberal model of a global market society beyond
  the state already mentioned;

- the post-Marxist scenario of a dispersed empire without a power center; and
- the anti-Kantian project of a system of hemispheres polemically affirming their incommensurable forms of life in opposition to one another.

The neoliberal model of global market society anticipates a progressive marginalization of state and politics. Politics retains at most the residual functions of the night watchman state,[109] whereas international law above the level of the state mutates into a global system of private law that institutionalizes trade and commerce. The rule of self-executing laws can dispense with state sanctions because the coordinating functions of global markets can assure a pre-political integration of world society. The marginalized states will regress to just one type of functional system among others because the depoliticization of private citizens renders the functions of political socialization and civic identity-formation superfluous. The global human rights regime is restricted to the negative liberties of citizens who acquire an "immediate" status vis-à-vis the global economy.[110]

This vision, which was in vogue in the 1990s, has in the meantime been overtaken by the return of a Hobbesian security regime and by the explosive character of politicized religions. The image of an apolitical global market society no longer coheres with a world stage on which international terrorism has made its appearance and religious fundamentalism is reviving forgotten political categories: the "axis of evil" also transforms opponents into enemies. But the brave new world of neoliberalism has not only been rendered empirically null and void; normatively speaking it was a non-starter, for it robs individuals of their status as citizens and abandons them to the contingencies of an unmanageably complex society. The individual liberties of private legal subjects are merely threads on which autonomous citizens dangle like puppets.

From the perspective of critics of globalization, the post-Marxist scenario of a dispersed imperial power illuminates the reverse side of the neoliberal project. It shares the latter's rejection of the classical image of state-centered politics but not the counter-image of the global peace of a bustling private law society. It sees private legal relations beyond the state as the ideological expression of the dynamics of an anonymous power that prises open ever-wider cleavages within the anarchistic global society between vampiristic centers and desiccated peripheries. The global dynamic has become detached from interactions among states, but this self-propelling system can no longer be identified exclusively with the global economy.[111] Self-reproducing capital is replaced by a kind of vague expressive power that penetrates base and superstructure alike and manifests itself in cultural as well as economic and military violence.[112] The correlate of the decentering of power is the local character of the dispersed forms of resistance that oppose it.

This conceptually vague scenario finds support in the superficial evidence that state power is becoming de-differentiated in a world society marked by growing social disparities and deepening cultural fragmentation as a result of the globalization of the economy and the media. This highly speculative outlook, though it may be fruitful for social science, has nothing much to offer to a diagnosis of the future of international law because the limited conceptual frame prevents it from taking account of the intrinsic normative dynamics of legal development.[113] The distinctive dialectic of the history of international law cannot be interpreted with a completely deformalized conception of law as a mere reflection of underlying power constellations. The egalitarian and individualistic universalism of human rights and democracy has a "logic" that interferes with the dynamics of power.

Carl Schmitt took issue with this universalistic presupposition of the Kantian project throughout his career. Hence, his critique of international law is gaining new adherents among those who contest the priority of the right over the good on contextualist grounds or who suspect, for reasons grounded in the critique of reason, that universalistic discourse is always a mask for particular interests. Informed by this moral non-cognitivism, Schmitt's diagnosis appears to offer an explanation for current trends, such as the detachment of politics from the state and the political relevance of cultural hemispheres that transcend state boundaries.

Kant or Schmitt?

In his capacity as an international lawyer, Carl Schmitt developed essentially two arguments. The first is directed against a "discriminatory concept of war" and any further juridification of international relations; the other argument, the replacement of states by imperial hemispheres, is an attempt to salvage the supposed merits of classical international law beyond the dissolution of the European state system.

With his defense of the legitimacy of war in international law, Schmitt was reacting, on the one hand, to the League of Nations and the Kellogg-Briand Pact and, on the other, to the question of war guilt raised by the Versailles Peace Treaty. For only if war is prohibited by international law can a warring government incur "guilt." Schmitt defended the classical principle of international law that states cannot do anything wrong in a moral sense with an argument he shared with Hans Morgenthau: judging opponents in moral terms poisons international relations and intensifies wars. He made the universalistic peace ideal of the Wilsonian League of Nations responsible for the fact "that the distinction between just and unjust wars brings about an increasingly radical and acute, a more 'total' distinction between friend and foe."[114]

Because he thinks that conceptions of justice necessarily remain controversial between states, there can be no justice between nations. This view rests on the assumption that normative arguments in international relations are nothing more than a pretext for masking one's own interests. The moralizing party is seeking to promote its own advantage by unfairly denigrating its opponent; contesting one's opponent's status as an honorable enemy, or *justus hostis*, produces an asymmetrical relation between parties that are in principle equal. Worse still, the moralization of war previously regarded as morally indifferent aggravates the conflict and leads to the "degeneration" of the conduct of war which is at least domesticated by law. After World War II, Schmitt radicalized his argument further in a legal opinion for the defense of Friedrich Flick before the Nuremberg Tribunal;[115] evidently, the "atrocities" of total war[116] could do nothing to shake his faith in the blamelessness of the subjects of international law.

Once we conceive the ban on war as a step toward the "juridification" of international relations, it becomes apparent that Schmitt's complaint about the "moralization" of war is beside the point. For the consequence of this move is to replace the distinction between just and unjust wars, whether grounded in natural law or in religion, by the procedural distinction between legal and illegal wars. Legal wars thereby take on the significance of global police operations. With the establishment of an international criminal court and the codification of the relevant crimes, positive law would be extended to the international level and, under the protection of legal due process, also safeguard the accused from moral prejudgments.[117] The recent conflict within the Security Council over the absence of evidence of weapons of mass destruction in Iraq and the continuation of weapons inspections made clear, at any rate, the role procedures can play in questions of war and peace.

On Schmitt's understanding, legal pacifism leads inevitably to excesses of violence because he tacitly assumed that any attempt to domesticate military violence by legal means must fail. He was convinced that competing conceptions of justice are incommensurable. Competing states or nations cannot agree on a single conception of justice, and certainly not on the liberal concepts of democracy and human rights. However, Schmitt never provided any philosophical justification for this thesis.[118] His non-cognitivism rests instead on an existential "concept of the political."[119] He believed in an irreducible antagonism between hypersensitive and aggressive nations that must assert their respective collective identities in opposition to one another. Schmitt's "social-ontological" antithesis to the Kantian conception of the juridification of international relations is grounded in this dimension. For him, the substance of "the political" always consisted in the disposition to violent self-assertion, which he initially understood in terms of the nation-state, then in fascistic-nationalistic terms, and finally in terms of a nebulous *Lebensphilosophie*. At all stages, however, his notion of "the political" was charged with fantasies of life and death struggles. Schmitt's opposition to the universalism of Kant's philosophy of law was primarily motivated by his rejection of the function of "rationalizing" the substance of political power which the constitution is supposed to perform both within the nation-state and in the international domain.

For Schmitt, the locus of the political was in the first instance the impervious irrational core of the bureaucratic authority of executive state agencies. The process of constitutional domestication must come to a halt before this core; otherwise, the state's capacity to assert itself against external and internal enemies would be impaired.[120] Schmitt inherited the idea of the "state behind the law" from an antiparliamentary ideology of legal positivism that prevailed in pre-World War I imperial Germany. This doctrine attributes to the state a "will of its own"; as it happens, through Schmitt's students it enjoyed a later career even among constitutional lawyers of the early Federal Republic of Germany during the 1950s. However, Schmitt himself had already detached his expressive-

190

dynamic conception of "the political" from the state during the 1930s. He first projected it onto the mobilized "people," the fascistically marshaled nation, and later onto partisans, liberation movements, the parties in civil wars, etc. Presumably, he would now also apply it to fanatical terrorist groups who perform suicide attacks: "Schmitt's emphatic defense of the political as a world of collectivities who demand a readiness to die of their members is ultimately driven by a fundamental moral critique of a world without transcendence and existential seriousness, of the 'dynamic of eternal competition and eternal discussion,' and of 'the faith in the masses of an antireligious secular activism'."[121]

Already in 1938, in the second edition of his work *Zum diskriminierenden Kriegsbegriff* (*On the Discriminatory Concept of War*), Schmitt distances himself from a conservative reading of his former critique of the prohibition of war in international law. In the meantime, he had embraced the idea of "total war" which he had previously denounced as the consequence of an ill-conceived humanitarian abolition of war. Hence, he could now reject any attempt to return to the classical international law of belligerent states as reactionary: "Our criticism [of the discriminatory conception of war] is not directed against the notion of fundamentally new orders."[122] In the middle of the war, in 1941, with the eastward expansion of the German Reich in view, Schmitt developed a forward-oriented, genuinely fascistic,[123] but after the war hastily de-Nazified, conception of international law.[124] This second argument takes up the constructive idea of a politics beyond the state. In response to his criticism of the Kantian project, he outlines a project of his own: a system of hemispheres is supposed to bind the otherwise dangerously proliferating political energies once again into an authoritarian form.

Schmitt chooses the 1823 Monroe Doctrine (suitably interpreted) as a model for an international legal construction that divides the world into territorial "hemispheres"

191

[*Großraüme*] shielded against the interventions of "alien powers" [*raumfremde Mächte*]: "The original Monroe Doctrine had the political meaning of defending a new political idea against the existing powers of the legitimate status quo by excluding interventions by alien powers."[125] On this model, the lines of demarcation laid down by international law define separate "spheres of sovereignty" conceived, not as state territories, but as "spheres of influence." These spheres are dominated by imperial powers and are shaped by the impact of their ideas. Internally, the "empires" are hierarchically ordered. Dependent nations and population groups within their territory submit to the authority of a "naturally" leading power that has achieved pre-eminence through its superior historical accomplishments. The status of a subject of international law is not granted automatically: "Not all peoples are capable of passing the test of creating a sound modern state apparatus and very few have the organizational, industrial and technical resources to conduct a modern war on their own."[126]

The international system of hemispheres transfers the principle of non-intervention to the spheres of influence of major powers who assert their cultures and forms of life against one another in a sovereign manner and, if necessary, with military force. The concept of "the political" is sublimated into the self-assertion and radiating influence of imperial powers who impose the stamp of their ideas, values, and national form of life on the identity of the hemisphere as a whole. Conceptions of justice are supposed to remain as incommensurable as before. The new international legal order does not find its guarantee, any more than did the classical, "in some substantive notion of justice, or in an international legal consciousness" – but in the "balance of powers."[127]

I have devoted so much space to this project of an international legal system of hemispheres, originally designed for the "Third Reich," because it is capable of acquiring a fatal zeitgeist appeal. The project links up with current trends toward the deformalization and delimitation of state power, while not playing down the enduring importance of political actors generally, as do the liberal and post-Marxist models. Schmitt anticipates the rise of continental regimes to which the Kantian project also assigns an important role. Moreover, his model invests the conception of hemispheres with connotations that accord with the current idea of a "clash of cultures." The design operates with an expressivist conception of power that has found resonance in postmodern theories and it corresponds to a pervasive skepticism concerning the possibility of intercultural dialogue over universally acceptable interpretations of human rights and democracy.

Based on this skepticism – for which the new cultural conflicts provide some misleading evidence but no cogent philosophical grounds – an updated theory of hemispheres offers itself as a not altogether implausible counterproposal to the hegemonic liberal model of unipolar global order. In Schmitt's case, it was already nourished by ressentiment against Western modernity and its updated versions remain completely blind to the productive ideas of self-consciousness, self-determination, and self-realization that continue to shape the normative self-understanding of modernity.

Notes

Editor's Preface

1 For Habermas's analysis of the interpretive problems posed by Kant's treatment of cosmopolitanism, see "Kant's Idea of Perpetual Peace: At Two Hundred Years' Historical Remove," in *The Inclusion of the Other*, ed. and trans. Ciaran Cronin and Pablo De Greiff (Cambridge: Polity, 1998), pp. 165–201.

2 Kant's well-founded concern that a world republic, thus conceived, would inevitably become "despotic" led him to weaken his cosmopolitan ideal considerably in practice (though not, as Habermas emphasizes, to abandon it altogether) and to advocate a voluntary "league of nations" as the only viable model for pacifying international political relations. The resulting apparent inconsistencies in his treatment have given rise to much controversy.

3 For Habermas's defense of the underlying principle of the co-originality of the *principle of popular sovereignty* and the *rule of law*, see especially Habermas, *Between Facts and Norms*, trans. William Rehg (Cambridge: Polity, 1996), chs. 3 and 4 and Appendix I, and *The Inclusion of the Other*, ch. 10.

4 Mindful of Schmitt's baleful influence on postwar German constitutional theory (and perhaps also, indirectly, on American neoconservatives), Habermas has punctuated his writings on cosmopolitanism and international law with sharp polemics against Carl Schmitt. See *The Inclusion of the Other*, pp. 134–43, 188–201; *The*

194

Postnational Constellation, ed. and trans. Max Pensky (Cambridge: Polity, 2001), p. 29; *Time of Transitions*, ed. and trans. Ciaran Cronin and Max Pensky (Cambridge: Polity, 2006), pp. 25–6; and this volume, pp. 19, 24, 105–6, 187–93.

5   See the essay "From Power Politics to Cosmopolitan Society," written three weeks into the NATO intervention when the problems of excessive military force and the lack of clear political goals had become apparent, in Habermas, *Time of Transitions*, pp. 19–30. Both then and subsequently, Habermas has insisted that the unilateralism of the NATO intervention should not be repeated.

6   See, in particular, Habermas, "The Postnational Constellation and the Future of Democracy," in *The Postnational Constellation*, pp. 58–112.

7   For Habermas's detailed analyses of the shifting constellations of political opinion within the European Union and their historical determinants, see *The Inclusion of the Other*, pp. 129–61; *The Postnational Constellation*, pp. 89–112; and *Time of Transitions*, pp. 73–109.

8   The recent eastern enlargement of the EU discussed by Habermas involved the accession of ten new, primarily Eastern European, member states on May 1, 2004. A "Draft Treaty Establishing a Constitution for Europe" was adopted by a convention on July 18, 2003, but it was initially blocked by the heads of state, precipitating the constitutional crisis to which Habermas refers (pp. 64–5, 71ff.). In the meantime, the draft constitution was adopted by the heads of the member states in Rome on October 29, 2004, but the French and Dutch electorates failed to ratify it in referenda in May and June, 2005, thus aggravating further the constitutional crisis.

9   See, in addition to chs. 3 and 6 of this volume, *The Inclusion of the Other*, ch. 6 and *Time of Transitions*, ch. 7.

Chapter 1   Fundamentalism and Terror

1   The interview was conducted in December 2001 by Giovanna Borradori, who teaches philosophy at Vassar College.

2 Beginning on September 18, 2001, a series of letters containing deadly anthrax spores, probably originating from US biological weapons research laboratories, were mailed to various media organizations and to two US senators, resulting in five deaths. Investigations of the crime have remained inconclusive. On November 12, 2001, American Airlines Flight 587 crashed into a residential area of Queens shortly after taking off from Kennedy International Airport, killing 265 people. The cause of the crash has been officially attributed to a technical failure due to pilot error. (Ed.).

3 The conference in question took place in late November and early December 2001. It brought together representatives of the various factions of the Northern Alliance, which played a leading role in the US-led campaign against the Taliban regime, and a number of Afghan exile groups to negotiate an agreement on the political future of the country with UN mediation. (Ed.).

4 United States Department of Defense, "Statement as Delivered by Secretary of Defense Donald H. Rumsfeld, Brussels, Belgium, December 18, 2001" (www.defenselink.mil/speeches/2001/s20011218-secdef1.html).

5 See Habermas, "Glaube, Wissen – Öffnung," *Süddeutsche Zeitung*, October 15, 2001 (a speech delivered on receiving the Peace Prize of the German Book Trade in Frankfurt). (Ed.).

6 Karl Jaspers coined the term "Axial Age" [*Achsenzeit*] to refer to the period from 800 to 200 BCE during which the major advances underlying later civilization occurred concurrently and independently in China, India, the Orient, and the West. (Ed.).

Chapter 2 Interpreting the Fall of a Monument

1 See the documentation by Stefan Frölich in the *Frankfurter Allgemeine Zeitung*, April 10, 2003.

Chapter 3 February 15, or: What Binds Europeans

1 This essay was published jointly with Jacques Derrida as part of an initiative in which Umberto Eco, Adolf Muschg, Richard Rorty, Fernando Savater, and Gianni Vattimo participated simultaneously in a number of European newspapers.
2 See Derrida, *Rogues: Two Essays on Reason* (Stanford, CA: Stanford University Press, 2005). (Ed.).
3 See Giovanna Borradori, *Philosophy in a Time of Terror: Dialogues with Jürgen Habermas and Jacques Derrida* (Chicago: University of Chicago Press, 2003), which contains interviews and essays by Habermas and Derrida. (Ed.).

Chapter 4 Core Europe as Counterpower? Follow-up Questions

1 The interview was conducted by Albrecht von Lucke for the journal *Blätter für deutsche und internationale Politik*.
2 The question is referring, respectively, to the essays reprinted in chs. 3 and 2 of this collection. (Ed.).
3 Rorty's article "Humiliation or Solidarity? The Hope for a Common European Foreign Policy" (*Dissent* 50/4 (Fall 2003): 23–6) was his contribution to the initiative launched by Habermas and Derrida in the appeal documented in ch. 3 above. (Ed.).
4 See Jürgen Habermas, *Autonomy and Solidarity*, ed. Peter Dews (London: Verso, 1992), p. 241.
5 I.e. ch. 3 above. (Ed.).

Chapter 5 The State of German–Polish Relations

1 The interview was conducted in December 2003 following the failed "constitutional summit" in Brussels by the Berlin correspondent of the Warsaw review "Gazeta," Anna Rupinowicz-Gründler.

2 On October 3, 2003, Martin Hohmann, a member of parliament for the conservative CDU party, delivered an anti-Semitic speech in which he described the Jews as a "perpetrator people" (*Tätervolk*), referring to alleged crimes of Jewish members of the Communist Party and the secret police during the Russian Revolution. The resulting scandal was aggravated by the fact that the leader of the CDU, Angela Merkel, took almost a month to distance herself publicly from Hohmann. Hohmann was dismissed from the parliamentary faction of the CDU and was later expelled from the party. The affair acquired wider significance when a general of the *Bundeswehr* was dismissed for congratulating Hohmann on his speech in a leaked private communication. (Ed.).

3 In late 1992 and early 1993 a number of racially motivated attacks were committed by right-wing groups in Germany, culminating in a firebomb attack on a house in Solingen on May 29, 1993, in which five Turkish women and girls were killed. (Ed.).

4 The League of Expellees (*Bund der Vertriebenen*) was founded in 1958 as a national umbrella organization for associations representing the interests of various groups of ethnic Germans who were expelled or otherwise displaced from Eastern European countries at the end of World War II. Its current president, Erica Steinbach, a member of parliament for the CDU, has sought multiparty support for an initiative to found a Center against Expulsions in Berlin. Its declared goal is to place the expulsions of Germans in the context of other twentieth-century expulsions, though it would remain under the exclusive control of the League of Expellees. Her initiative has met with vigorous opposition in neighboring Eastern European countries, especially Poland. (Ed.).

Chapter 6   Is the Development of a European Identity Necessary, and Is It Possible?

1 Georg Vobruba, "The Enlargement Crisis of the European Union," *Journal of European Social Policy* 13 (2003): 35–57.

2 I owe this reference to a lecture of Claus Offe, "Sozialpolitik und internationale Politik. Über zwei Hindernisse auf dem Wege zum 'Zusammenhalt' Europas" (Ms., October 2002).

3 See the interview with Joschka Fischer in the *Frankfurter Allgemeine Zeitung*, March 6, 2004, p. 9.

4 Here I am alluding to a fear expressed by Heinrich Schneider (in a lecture on core Europe held in January 2004). (See Schneider, "'Kerneuropa' – ein aktuelles Schlagwort und seine Bedeutung," *EI Working Papers* 54 (February 2004) (http://epub.wu-wien.ac.at/dyn/virlib/wp/showentry?ID=epub-wu-01_6d1). (Ed.).)

5 Hauke Brunkhorst, "Verfassung ohne Staat?," *Leviathan* 30/4 (2004): 530–43.

6 Michael Zürn, "Democratic Governance beyond the Nation-State: The EU and Other International Institutions," *European Journal of International Relations* 6 (2000): 183–221.

7 See note 3 above.

Chapter 7   An Interview on War and Peace

1 This interview was conducted by Eduardo Mendieta (Department of Philosophy, SUNY, Stony Brook).

2 See above, ch. 1, p. 6.

3 See Habermas, "From Power Politics to Cosmopolitan Society," in *Time of Transitions*, ed. and trans. Ciaran Cronin and Max Pensky (Cambridge: Polity, 2006), p. 30.

4 See above, ch. 3, pp. 39–40.

5 On April 9, 2003, US troops entered Baghdad and toppled a statue of Saddam Hussein in a scene immediately relayed around the world by television. For Habermas's remarks on its significance, see above, pp. 26ff. (Ed.).

6 See Robert Kagan, *Of Paradise and Power: America and Europe in the New World Order* (New York: Knopf, 2003). (Ed.).

7 As it happens, the November 2004 presidential elections in the United States, to which Habermas is referring, did not lead to a change in administration, since George W.

Bush defeated his Democratic Party challenger John Kerry. (Ed.).

8 On September 5, 1977, the Red Army Faction abducted and later murdered the industrialist Hans Martin Schleyer in Cologne. The socialist-liberal coalition government under Helmut Schmidt responded to the abduction and a subsequent airplane hijacking with harsh security measures, thereby contributing to a mood of crisis and instability. (Ed.).

9 For Walzer's critical assessment of the hegemonic unilateralism underlying the policies of the Bush administration, see Michael Walzer, "Is there an American Empire?" *Dissent* 50/4 (Fall 2003): 27–31. (Ed.).

10 See below, ch. 8, p. 171. (Ed.).

Chapter 8 Does the Constitutionalization of International Law Still Have a Chance?

1 I am indebted to Hauke Brunkhorst for stimulating discussions during the preparation of this text and to Arnim von Bogdandy for helpful comments on the penultimate version.

2 Bardo Fassbender, "The United Nations Charter as Constitution of the International Community," *Columbia Journal of Transnational Law* 36 (1998): 529–619; Jochen A. Frowein, "Konstitutionalisierung des Volkerrechts," in *Völkerrecht und internationales Recht in einem sich globalisierenden internationalen System*, Berichte der Deutschen Gesellschaft für Völkerrecht 39 (Heidelberg: Müller, 2000), pp. 427–47; for a more comprehensive treatment, see Hauke Brunkhorst, *Solidarität. Von der Bürgerfreundschaft zur globalen Rechtsgenossenschaft* (Frankfurt am Main: Suhrkamp Verlag, 2000); Brun-Otto Bryde, "Konstitutionalisierung des Völkerrechts und Internationalisierung des Verfassungsrechts," *Der Staat* 42 (2003): 62–75.

3 Ernst-Otto Czempiel, *Weltpolitik im Umbruch* (Munich: Beck, 1993).

4 Czempiel, *Neue Sicherheit in Europa. Eine Kritik an Neorealismus und Realpolitik* (Frankfurt am Main: Campus, 2002).

5 Thomas L. Pangle and Peter J. Ahrensdorf, *Justice among Nations* (Lawrence, Kan.: University Press of Kansas, 1999).
6 See Kant, *The Conflict of the Faculties*, trans. Mary Gregor (New York: Abaris Books, 1979), p. 169: "[human beings] will see themselves compelled to render the greatest obstacle to morality – that is to say, war . . . – firstly by degrees more humane and then rarer, and finally to renounce offensive war altogether.".
7 Kant, "Toward Perpetual Peace: A Philosophical Project," in Kant, *Practical Philosophy*, ed. and trans. Mary Gregor (Cambridge: Cambridge University Press, 1996), p. 328.
8 Philip Kunig, "Völkerrecht und staatliches Recht," in Wolfgang Graf Vitzthum, *Völkerrecht*, 2nd edn. (Berlin: de Gruyter, 2001), pp. 87–160.
9 Kant, "On the Common Saying: That May Be Correct in Theory but it is of No Use in Practice," in Kant, *Practical Philosophy*, p. 309.
10 Kant, "Toward Perpetual Peace," p. 318.
11 Kant, *The Metaphysics of Morals*, ed. and trans. Mary Gregor (Cambridge: Cambridge University Press, 1996), p. 123.
12 Volker Gerhardt, *Immanuel Kants Entwurf "Zum ewigen Frieden"* (Darmstadt: Wissenschaftliche Buchgesellschaft, 1995).
13 Kant, *Metaphysics of Morals*, pp. 123, 121 (translation amended).
14 Kant, "Idea for a Universal History with a Cosmopolitan Intent," in Kant, *Perpetual Peace and Other Essays*, trans. Ted Humphrey (Indianapolis: Hackett, 1983), p. 34.
15 Kant, *Metaphysics of Morals*, p. 30.
16 Ingeborg Maus, *Zur Aufklärung der Demokratietheorie* (Frankfurt am Main: Suhrkamp Verlag, 1992), pp. 176ff.
17 Jürgen Habermas, *Between Facts and Norms*, trans. William Rehg (Cambridge, Mass.: MIT Press, 1996), pp. 133ff.
18 Kant, "Idea for a Universal History," pp. 34–5.
19 Kant, "Theory and Practice," p. 295.
20 Kant, "Conclusion" to "Doctrine of Right," in *Metaphysics of Morals*, p. 123.

21   Kant, "Toward Perpetual Peace," p. 328.

22   Cf. Kant, "Theory and Practice," p. 309.

23   Ibid., p. 308. So too the later work "Toward Perpetual Peace," p. 322n., where Kant relates cosmopolitan law to persons "regarded as citizens of a universal state of mankind."

24   Kant, "Toward Perpetual Peace," p. 328 (translation amended).

25   I was first convinced of this by Thomas A. McCarthy, "On Reconciling Cosmopolitan Unity and National Diversity," in Pablo de Greiff and Ciaran Cronin, eds., *Global Justice and Transnational Politics* (Cambridge, Mass.: MIT Press, 2002), pp. 235–74.

26   For a more in-depth discussion, see Habermas, "Kant's Idea of Perpetual Peace: At Two Hundred Years' Historical Remove," in idem., *The Inclusion of the Other*, ed. and trans. Ciaran Cronin and Pablo de Greiff (Cambridge, Mass.: MIT Press, 1998), pp. 165–201.

27   Kant, "Toward Perpetual Peace," p. 330 (translation modified).

28   Ibid., p. 326.

29   See the contributions of Reinhard Brandt, Volker Gerhardt, Otfried Höffe, and Wolfgang Kersting, in Höffe, ed., *Immanuel Kant: Zum Ewigen Frieden* (Berlin: Akademie Verlag, 1995); also: Brandt, "Historisch-kritische Beobachtungen zu Kants Friedensschrift," in Reinhard Merkel and Roland Wittmann, eds., *Zum Ewigen Frieden* (Frankfurt am Main: Suhrkamp, 2001), pp. 12–30; Orlando Budelacci, *Kants Friedensprogramm* (Bamberg: Athena, 2003).

30   Kersting, "Globale Rechtsordnung oder weltweite Verteilungsgerechtigkeit?" in *Recht, Gerechtigkeit und demokratische Tugend* (Frankfurt am Main: Suhrkamp Verlag, 1997), pp. 243–315: here p. 269.

31   Stefan Oeter, "Souveränität und Demokratie als Problem der Verfassungsentwicklung der Europäischen Union," *Zeitschrift für ausländisches öffentliches Recht und Völkerrecht* 55/3: 659–712.

32   See the "Conclusion" to "Doctrine of Right," in *Metaphysics of Morals*, pp. 123–4.

33 Kant, "Theory and Practice," p. 307.
34 I am indebted for this point to Pauline Kleingeld, *Kant's Theory of Peace* (Ms. 2004).
35 Habermas, *Between Facts and Norms*, pp. 133–51.
36 Cf. Maus, *Zur Aufklärung der Demokratietheorie.*
37 On the concept of a federal world republic, see Otfried Höffe, *Demokratie im Zeitalter der Globalisierung* (Munich: C. H. Beck, 1999); Stephen Gosepath and Jean-Christoph Merle, eds., *Weltrepublik: Globalisierung und Demokratie* (Munich: C. H. Beck, 2002).
38 Michael Greven and Rainer Schmalz-Bruns, eds., *Politische Theorie – heute* (Baden-Baden: Nomos, 1999), Part III; Beata Kohler-Koch, ed., *Regieren in entgrenzten Räumen*, Politische Vierteljahresschrift, 39 (1998); Markus Jachtenfuchs and Michele Knodt, eds., *Regieren in internationalen Organizationen* (Opladen: Leske & Budrich, 2002).
39 Habermas, *The Postnational Constellation*, trans. Max Pensky (Cambridge: Polity, 2001), pp. 104–12.
40 Brunkhorst, "Globale Solidarität: Inklusionsprobleme moderner Gesellschaften," in Lutz Wingert and Klaus Günther, eds., *Die Öffentlichkeit der Vernunft und die Vernunft der Öffentlichkeit* (Frankfurt am Main: Suhrkamp Verlag, 2001), pp. 605–26; "Globalising Democracy without a State," *Millennium Journal of International Studies* 31/3 (2002): 675–90; *Demokratie in der globalen Rechtsgenossenschaft. Zeitschrift für Soziologie*, Sonderheft Weltgesellschaft (forthcoming).
41 Christoph Möllers shows how in European constitutional law the liberal constitutional idea of "restricting authority" becomes connected with the genuinely democratic constitutional idea of "founding authority." See Möllers, "Verfassungsgebende Gewalt – Verfassung – Konstitutionalisierung. Begriffe der Verfassung in Europa," in Arnim von Bogdandy, ed., *Europäisches Verfassungsrecht* (Berlin: Springer, 2003), pp. 1–56.
42 Günter Frankenberg, "Die Rückkehr des Vertrages. Überlegungen zur Verfassung der Europäischen Union," in Wingert and Günther, eds., *Die Öffentlichkeit der Vernunft*, pp. 507–38.

43 Bryde, "Konstitutionalisierung des Völkerrechts," p. 62.
44 Habermas, *Between Facts and Norms*, pp. 118–31; "On the Internal Relation between the Rule of Law and Democracy," in *The Inclusion of the Other*, pp. 253–64; "Constitutional Democracy: A Paradoxical Union of Contradictory Principles?" *Political Theory* 29/6 (2001): 766–81.
45 Rudolf Dolzer, "Wirtschaft und Kultur im Völkerrecht," in Vitzthum, *Völkerrecht*, pp. 502–19.
46 See the *Special Report on the WTO Cancun Ministerial* of September 16, 2003 (www.globalservicesnetwork.com/pdf/PostCancun.pdf).
47 Brunkhorst, "Globalising Democracy without a State."
48 Kant, "Toward Perpetual Peace," p. 336n.
49 Gilbert Guillaume, "Terrorism and International Law," *International and Comparative Law Quarterly* 53 (2004): 537–48.
50 I owe this point to Nico Krisch, *Imperial Law* (Ms. 2003).
51 Cf. the useful survey in Arnim von Bogdandy, "Demokratie, Globalisierung, Zukunft des Völkerrechts – eine Bestandaufnahme," in *Zeitschrift für ausländisches und öffentliches Recht und Völkerrecht* 63/4 (2003): 852–77.
52 There has been no shortage of attempts to save Hegel's honour; see, most recently, Robert Fine, "Kant's Theory of Cosmopolitanism and Hegel's Critique," *Philosophy & Social Criticism* 29/6 (2003): 611–32.
53 Friedrich Wilhelm August Fröbel (1782–1852), who was influenced by the Rousseauean educational reformer Johann Heinrich Pestalozzi, founded the kindergarten movement. (Ed.).
54 A photomechanical reprint was published in 1975 by Scientia Verlag, Aalen: Julius Fröbel, *System der sozialen Politik*, 2nd edn. (Mannheim 1847; hereinafter Fröbel (1847), vols. I and II). The biographical details are adapted from Rainer Koch's introduction to this reprint.
55 Cf. Habermas, "Popular Sovereignty as Procedure," in *Between Facts and Norms*, pp. 463–90: here pp. 473ff.
56 I.e. the period of political ferment in the German states leading up to failed revolutions of March 1848. (Ed.).

57 Fröbel (1847), vol. II, p. 458.
58 Fröbel (1847), vol. I, pp. 246f.
59 Ibid., p. 245.
60 Ibid., p. 538.
61 Ibid., p. 57.
62 Fröbel (1847), vol. II, p. 469.
63 Fröbel (1847), vol. I, p. 250.
64 Fröbel (1847), vol. II, pp. 462ff.
65 His sensitization to the race question in the USA had even transformed the renegade into a precursor of social Darwinism.
66 A photomechanical reprint of the Vienna edition appeared in the Scientia Verlag, Aalen, in 1975: Julius Fröbel, *Theorie der Politik* (Vienna, 1861: hereinafter Fröbel (1861), vols. I and II).
67 Fröbel (1861), vol. I, p. 331.
68 Ibid., p. 328.
69 Lasson, *Prinzip und Zukunft des Völkerrechts* (Berlin 1871).
70 Martti Koskenniemi, *The Gentle Civilizer of Nations. The Rise and Fall of International Law 1870–1960* (Cambridge: Cambridge University Press, 2002), pp. 179–265.
71 Ibid., p. 87.
72 Hans Kelsen and Carl Schmitt engaged in debates with George Scelle and Hersch Lauterpacht.
73 Thomas Knock, *To End all Wars: Woodrow Wilson and the Quest for a New World Order* (Princeton, NJ: Princeton University Press, 1995), ch. 4.
74 Gerhard Beestermöller, *Die Völkerbundsidee* (Stuttgart: Kohlhammer, 1997), pp. 16ff.
75 Ibid., pp. 101ff.
76 Woodrow Wilson, *The Public Papers of Woodrow Wilson*, ed. Ray Stannard Baker and William E. Dodd, vol. I (New York: Harper and Brothers, 1925), p. 233.
77 Alfred Verdross and Bruno Simma, *Universelles Völkerrecht*, 3rd edn. (Berlin: Duncker & Humblot, 1984), pp. 66ff.
78 Bryde, "Konstitutionalisierung des Völkerrechts und Internationalisierung des Verfassungsrechts," p. 62.
79 Fassbender, "The United Nations Charter as Constitution of the International Community," lists eight constitutive

characteristics of a constitution: "A Constitutive Moment, System of Governance, Definition of Membership, Hierarchy of Norms, 'Eternity' and Amendment, A 'Charter,' Constitutional History, Universality and the Problem of Sovereignty."

80   On the internationalization of human rights, see Hauke Brunkhorst, Wolfgang R. Köhler, and Matthias Lutz-Bachmann, eds., *Recht auf Menschenrechte* (Frankfurt am Main: Suhrkamp Verlag, 1999).

81   Kay Hailbronner, "Der Staat und der Einzelne als Völkerrechtssubjekte," in Vitzthum, *Völkerrecht*, pp. 161–267.

82   Jochen A. Frowein and Nico Krisch, "Chapter VIII. Action with respect to Threats to the Peace, Breaches of the Peace, and Acts of Aggression," in Bruno Simma, ed., *The Charter of the United Nations. A Commentary*, 2nd edn. (Oxford: Oxford University Press, 2002), pp. 701–63.

83   Habermas, "Remarks on Legitimation through Human Rights," in *The Postnational Constellation*, pp. 113–29.

84   Bernhard Zangl and Michael Zürn, *Krieg und Frieden* (Frankfurt am Main: Suhrkamp, 2003), pp. 38–55.

85   Pangle and Ahrensdorf, *Justice among Nations*, pp. 218–38.

86   Here Morgenthau is following Carl Schmitt. Cf. Koskenniemi, "Carl Schmitt, Hans Morgenthau, and the Image of Law in International Relations," in Michael Byers, ed., *The Role of Law in International Politics* (Oxford: Oxford University Press, 2003), pp. 17–34.

87   Kahn, "American Hegemony and International Law," *Chicago Journal of International Law* 2 (2000): 1–18: here p. 13.

88   See above pp. 29–30. For the contrary view, see the review article by Nico Krisch, "Legality, Morality and the Dilemma of Humanitarian Intervention after Kosovo," *European Journal of International Law* 13/1 (2002): 323–35.

89   Frowein and Krisch, "Chapter VIII. Action with respect to Threats to the Peace," pp. 724ff.

90   Jacques Derrida, *Rogues: Two Essays on Reason* (Stanford, CA: Stanford University Press, 2005).

91 Frowein, "Konstitutionalisierung des Volkerrechts," pp. 429ff.; Zangl and Zürn, *Frieden und Krieg*, pp. 254ff.

92 Herfried Münkler, *Die neue Kriege* (Reinbeck bei Hamburg: Rowohlt, 2002), pp. 13ff.

93 Ibid.; Zangl and Zürn, *Frieden und Krieg*, pp. 172–205.

94 For an analysis of the different cultural milieus from which fundamentalist movements draw their various motivations, see Martin Riesebrodt, *Die Rückkehr der Religionen* (Munich: C. H. Beck, 2003), p. 35.

95 Peter Waldmann, *Terrorismus und Bürgerkrieg* (Munich: Murmann, 2003).

96 Cf. the proposal presented to the Security Council by the Committee on Intervention and State Sovereignty in December 2001. The proposal shifts the emphasis from a "right to intervene" to the "responsibility for protecting the population."

97 The UN budget amounts to approximately 4 percent of the annual budget of New York City. For details, see Edward Kwakwa, "The International Community, International Law and the United States," in Michael Byers and George Nolte, eds., *United States Hegemony and the Foundation of International Law* (Cambridge: Cambridge University Press, 2003), p. 39.

98 On the following, see Ulrich Beck, *Power in the Global Age*, trans. Kathleen Cross (Cambridge: Polity, 2005); David Held and Andrew McGrew, eds., *Governing Globalization* (Cambridge: Polity, 2002).

99 Klaus Günther, "Rechtspluralismus und universaler Code der Legalität: Globalisierung als rechtstheoretisches Problem," in Wingert and Günther, eds., *Die Öffentlichkeit der Vernunft und die Vernunft der Öffentlichkeit*, pp. 539–67; Klaus Günther and Shalini Randeria, "Recht, Kultur und Gesellschaft im Prozess der Globalisierung," in *Schriftenreihe der Werner Reimers Stiftung* 4 (Bad Homburg, 2001).

100 Michael Zürn, "Politik in der postnationalen Konstellation," in Christine Landfried, ed., *Politik in einer entgrenzten Welt* (Cologne: Verlag Wissenschaft und Politik, 2001), pp. 181–204; "Zu den Merkmalen postnationalen Politik," in Jachtenfuchs and Knodt, eds., *Regieren in internationalen Institutionen*, pp. 215–34.

101 On this social constructive understanding of the transformation in international relations, see Alexander Wendt, *Social Theory of International Relations* (Cambridge: Cambridge University Press, 1999).

102 In France, the debate between adherents of the nation-state and Eurofederalists is also sparked by this question; cf. Patrick Savidan, ed., *La République ou l'Europe?* (Paris: Le Livre de Poche, 2004).

103 Held, *Global Covenant: The Social Democratic Alternative to the Washington Consensus* (Cambridge: Polity, 2004), p. 58.

104 Jochen Hippler and Jeanette Schade, "US-Unilateralismus als Problem von internationaler Politik und Global Governance," in *INEF*, Universität Duisburg, vol. 70 (2003). Cf. also the contribution to Part VI Compliance, in Byers and Nolte, *United States Hegemony*, pp. 427–514.

105 See the manuscript of Nico Krisch (above n. 50).

106 Brad R. Roth, "Bending the Law, Breaking it, or Developing it. The United States and the Humanitarian Use of Force in the post-Cold War Era," in Byers and Nolte, *United States Hegemony*, pp. 232–63.

107 Jed Rubenfeld, "Two World Orders," *Prospect* (January 2004): 32–7; abridged version of Rubenfeld, "Unilateralism and Constitutionalism," in G. Nolte, ed., *American and European Constitutionalism, Part IV* (forthcoming).

108 Habermas, "Reply to Symposium Participants, Benjamin N. Cardozo School of Law," *Cardozo Law Review* 17/4–5 (1996): 1477–1557.

109 Jean-Marie Guéhenno, *The End of the Nation-State*, trans. Victoria Elliott (Minneapolis: Minnesota University Press, 1995).

110 Kahn, "American Hegemony," p. 5: "As international law expands from a doctrine of state relations to a regime of individual rights, it poses a direct challenge to the traditional, political self-conception of the nation-state. Human rights law imagines a world of depoliticised individuals, i.e. individuals whose identity and rights precede their political identifications. Similarly, the international law of commerce imagines a single, global market order

in which political divisions are irrelevant. In both the domain of rights and commerce, the state is reduced to a means, not an end."

111 Michael Hardt and Antonio Negri, *Empire* (Cambridge, Mass.: Harvard University Press, 2002).

112 Koskenniemi, "Comments on Chapters 1 and 2," in Byers and Nolte, *United States Hegemony*, p. 98: "Instead of making room for only a few non-governmental decision makers, I am tempted by the larger vision of Hardt and Negri that the world is in transit toward what they, borrowing from Michel Foucault, call a biopolitical Empire, an Empire that has no capital, that is ruled from no one spot but that is equally binding on Washington and Karachi, and all of us. In this image, there are no interests that arise from states – only interest-positions that are dictated by an impersonally, globally effective economic and cultural logic.".

113 Elsewhere Koskenniemi (*The Gentle Civilizer of Nations*, pp. 494ff.) accords the role of the intrinsic normativity of the law its full due with his judicious formulation "culture of formalism."

114 Schmitt, *Die Wendung zum diskriminierenden Kriegsbegriff* (Berlin: Duncker & Humblot, 1991 [1938]), p. 50.

115 Schmitt, *Das internationalrechtliche Verbrechen des Angriffskrieges*, ed. H. Quaritsch (Berlin: Duncker & Humblot, 1994).

116 Ibid., p. 16.

117 Günther, "Kampf gegen das Böse?," in *Kritische Justiz* 27 (2004): 135–57.

118 Thus there is no need to address the issue of cognitivism in ethics here; cf. Habermas, *Justification and Application: Remarks on Discourse Ethics*, trans. Ciaran Cronin (Cambridge, Mass.: MIT Press, 1993).

119 Reinhard Mehring, ed., *Carl Schmitt: Der Begriff des Politischen. Ein kooperativer Kommentar* (Berlin: Akademie, 2003).

120 Christoph Schönberger, "Der Begriff des Staates im Begriff des Politischen," in Mehring, ed., *Ein kooperativer Kommentar*, p. 21; cf. also Hauke Brunkhorst, "Der lange Schatten des Staatswillenspositivismus," *Leviathan* 31/3 (2003): 360–3.

121 Schönberger, "Der Begriff des Staates im Begriff des Politischen," p. 41.

122 Schmitt, *Die Wendung zum diskriminierenden Kriegsbegriff*, p. 53.

123 Schmitt, *Völkerrechtliche Großraumordnung* (Berlin: Duncker & Humblot, 1991 (1945)).

124 Schmitt, *Der Nomos der Erde im Völkerrecht des Jus Publicum Europäum* (Berlin: Duncker & Humblot, 1997 [1950]).

125 Schmitt, *Völkerrechtliche Großraumordnung*, p. 34.

126 Ibid., p. 59.

127 Ibid., p. 56.

Index

218